POLITICS AND HISTORY

13

POLITICS AND HISTORY

In the same series:

THE MEDICI WOMEN

introduction by
FRANCO CARDINI

ARNAUD

Literary ownership reserved
1st Italian edition: October 1993
2nd Italian edition: December 1995
3rd Italian edition: March 1997
1st English edition: June 1996
2nd English edition: March 1997

Cover by Marco Vergoni

© Copyright: Arnaud Ed. s.r.l.
   P.O Box 18259
   50129 Firenze

Printed by *Gramma* - Perugia

On the jacket:
Domenico Ghirlandaio, *Birth of St. John the Baptist*
Florence, Church of Santa Maria Novella

INDEX

* *N.B.*

   For a complete bibliography on the members of the House of the Medici, refer to:
   SERGIO CAMERANI, Bibliografia Medicea (Olschki, Firenze, 1964).

INTRODUCTION

The legend still surrounding the house of the Medici is a mixture of gold and tar. Ever since the fifteenth century, literature on the subject has abounded. At times it has been obsequious, at times partisan, at times eulogistic, triumphal and, let us face it, servile, at times denigrating, preconceived and, let us face it, slanderous. This has only clouded the issue, but, though it has not hindered serious, unperturbed scientific research (which has indeed been conducted, giving good results, too), it has retarded the diffusion throughout public opinion of the outcome of it all.

Both the huge series of exhibitions which were held in Florence and throughout Tuscany in 1980 (the one dedicated to the principate) and in 1992 (the quincentenary of Lorenzo the Magnificent's death) gave an opportunity for fresh study and further thorough research. In spite of everything, however, they could not be said to have dispelled the old spectres or quashed legends which, though wide-spread, are in fact thread-bare.

Besides, it is not easy to find one's way around so many discordant voices. On one hand, on the morrow of the thwarted Pazzi conspiracy of 1478, it was a sorry sight to see the great Politian and even the sublime Sandro Botticelli both stooping to rather degrading forms of cowardly offence against the defeated Pazzi family in flight (and they undoubtedly did so with glee, more out of true affection for Lorenzo than for partisanship' or adulation). But, however, it must needs be recognised that Vittorio Alfieri's heroic rage against the "Medici yoke" only fostered, from the Romantic up until contemporary ages, a constantly anti-historical, rhetorical and moralistic interpretation of those Medicean events which coincided with the change from Florence as a city-state (imperfect controller of most of Tuscany) to an absolute regional one. But nineteenth-century, historically-romanticised literature and certain theatrical and cinematographic works at the beginning of this century have contributed to bolster heroic, super-human images of the long Medicean domination (or else sulphurous and degrading ones) and spread them around. Suffice it to consider the great quantity of less than mediocre literature that has been churned out concerning Duke Alessandro and "Lorenzaccio" (or "Lorenziano") in a contest of wit which has often been anything but mediocre, from Alfieri to De Musset up to Benelli and to Upton. Or indeed consider also the durability of the black legend surrounding the deaths of Giovanni and Garçia de' Medici (sons of Grand Duke Cosimo I) and Eleonora de Toledo, their mother. This chain of deceases occurred between 20 November and 18 December 1562 owing to a series of causes, the main one being the fever contracted in the Maremma district. Even in places where they should know better on this subject, the version is still nonchalantly doled out of the murder of Giovanni at the hands of Garçia and the subsequent ferocious execution of the fratricide which was carried out by an irate father under the eyes of Garçia's mother, even though he had come to beg their forgiveness.

Well, what about their mother? From so many portraits, Duchess Eleonora de Toledo, daughter of Don Pedro (the celebrated viceroy of Naples) surveys us solemnly in her jewelled attire, though, indeed, she is not always florid and serene. The most famous is perhaps Bronzino's lovely medallion in one of the two lunettes in Francesco I's "Studiolo". The stern, haughty lady who spoke but a little, halting Italian (and unwillingly at that) was not much loved by the Florentines who had, in any case, never really cared for the Medici clan. Though unobtrusively and reservedly, she, too, in no moderate manner, took part in Tuscan political life and in her husband's choices. And in times such as ours, when there is a renewed interest in women and their role, and there is an attempt also at a methodological definition of "women's history" as a historical discipline beset with its own problems, we must turn to many other ladies of the house of Medici in order to better appreciate the history of the dynasty and of Tuscany and Italy between the fifteenth and eighteenth centuries.

This book does not specifically concern scholars, who have their own instruments, rites and also, to a small degree, their manias. The aim is to present a few of the Medici women in the twofold intent of trying to rectify a few commonplaces and clarify the truth of some facts which are well-known on an analytical plane but to a minor extent on the plane of synthesis. We shall, therefore, see a rapid procession of ladies of the age of the Medicean republic. There is Tessa Bardi, wife of Cosimo the Elder, in these pages present only under the guise of a hovering spirit in the rooms of Via Larga, and then Lucrezia Tornabuoni, an energetic woman, cultured as she was pious, who bore the same name as Lucrezia Donati about whom we still know too little (though perhaps it is not worth our while to find out more). From the pages of this book arise the following personalities, justly reconsidered (and, if you wish, revalued): Clarice Orsini, Lorenzo the Magnificent's patient, austere consort; Bianca Cappello, wrongly slandered for generations; Catherine de' Medici, who was something other than a sorceress and over-protective mother; and Marie de' Medici who was not, perhaps, that gross schemer as described in certain historiography. Then there was Anna Maria Luisa, daughter of Grand Duke Cosimo III (who was perhaps treated rather too severely by his friend Furio Diaz) and of Marguerite-Louise d'Orléans (there was hardly any deep feeling between the two, but obviously they had at some time consorted, even though fleetingly). Anna Maria Luisa had inherited her mother's large eyes and heavy mass of chestnut hair and, though soon abandoned by her, could, however, take advantage of the guidance and affection offered by her paternal grandmother, Vittoria Della Rovere (another "Medici lady": Ah, these great families! as Jacques Prévert would have said...). She grew up haughty, profoundly religious and fond of pomp and luxury. So it was that in 1691, at the age of twenty-four, she embarked on her happy marriage to William, Elector Palatine of the Rhine. Relations with Spain had already ceased at that time and those with France were on the decline with Louis XIV's too lengthy reign giving way to the slump and pending crisis. For Tuscany and the house of Medici, the road towards Central Europe was opening up. The "baroque"-style mourning into which the Electress Palatine closed herself on the morrow of her husband's death in 1716 onwards (while her brother, Gian Gastone, followed *his* "baroque" destiny) is almost a symbol of the change that Europe underwent at the beginning of the eighteenth century and of the advent of new times.

FRANCO CARDINI

PREFACE

The Medici women, the subject of a series of lectures organised by the Florentine Lyceum, are here presented in the historical profiles in this collection.

The times referred to are those of the golden years of the house of the Medici, dating from the abatement of the democracy of the Communes, through the oligarchy and the Signoria as far as the Principate.

From the Middle Ages right up to the Modern Age, there have been other banking and merchant families in Europe which have exceeded the Medicis in wealth and economic activity, but not one has outstripped them in the contribution they made to civilisation with their political acumen and the enlightened patronage which had its outlet in the culture of which Florence was lord and master.

Did the Medici women contribute to this achievement?

The democracy of the Commune had changed the moral and juridical standing of women and had elevated it from the state it was in, still subject to the effect on customs and institutions caused by the aftermath of the feudal Middle Ages. Lorenzo the Magnificent's mother, wholly involved in procuring tutors for her son's education, is a worthy representative of this revolution which preluded the Renaissance. The Medici women provide true documentation of this; both directly and indirectly they contributed to this work of civilisation. Lorenzo dei Medici's women knew how to turn themselves out, how to dance, sing and give pleasure. They were also a sign of the transformation under way which they themselves participated in. And in the field of politics? Only Catherine, Queen of France, has a high historical profile among the Medici ladies. She showed skill in dominating a difficult political situation, and the preservation of the unity of France is in no small way due to her contribution.

But there is a feat achieved silently and under cover by the ladies of the House of Medici. Such is the case of Eleonora de Toledo, Duchess of Florence and Siena. Her politically-generated marriage had a solid base in the couple's reciprocal love. Eleonora's words to Cosimo were animated by this love, while he was intent on constructing the State and consolidating the political power of the new sovereign.

The small world of the Medici women must be viewed with a humanly sympathetic eye; here can be found grief, anxiety, pain, human flaws, culpability and fragility; in fact, the world we live in now. This sympathy has been the common undertaking of the authors of these historic profiles. First of all, Piero Bargellini comes forward with Lorenzo's women, presenting them with that Florentine self-possession which is a characteristic of his and which is art. Arnaldo D'Addario traces the profile of Eleonora de Toledo, sustains the documentation sifted through by the experts and agrees with the valuation of Eleonora as a wise, sovereign woman. It was difficult to put over the figure of Bianca Cappello without tripping up on commonplaces. Pina Marzi Ciotti has managed admirably, conducting her appeal case with serene judgement and psychological finesse. Pages full of spice are dedicated to Catherine and Marie de' Medici by Carlo Pellegrini, a discerning, authority on French history and literature. The rather unfortunate Maria Vittoria Della Rovere is described with intelligent insight by Lea Nissim Rossi. No-one could have thrown more light upon the sensitive, generous figure of the Electress Palatine than Anna Maria Ciaranfi.

Finally, a perspicacious Sergio Camerani narrates the life of Marguerite-Louise d'Orleans, wife of Cosimo III. He opens the windows of the Pitti Palace and, from a historical point of view, looks at Florence and Tuscany at the time of Cosimo III. The Tuscan genius did not wane in the murky twilight of the Medicean Principate. It was precisely at that time that the seeds of a new life were preparing a renewed Tuscany for the reforms of the eighteenth century; the genetic elements, however, can be traced back to the ill-famed Medicean Seicento.

NICCOLÒ RODOLICO

The Literature Section of the Florentine Lyceum has had the custom for some years now of holding a cycle of lectures on subjects concerning literature or history. The choice one year fell on "The Medici Women". So it was that, before the eyes of an attentive, constantly crowded audience, there paraded various figures of wise and prudent women, of dissolute princesses, of aristocratic ladies, of adventuresses, of young, pious girls and elderly bigots. In the background lay a historical Florence which, over a span of three centuries, offered a steadfastly compelling display of life and customs, with an array of personalities making a worthy frame around these leading ladies. Following the great success enjoyed by these lectures, Casa Editrice Arnaud has undertaken their publication, enriching the enterprise with numerous illustrations. We are confident that the reading public will warmly welcome this book, in the same way as the listeners at the Lyceum received the lectures.

LEA ROSSI NISSIM
President of the Literature Section of the Lyceum

THE LADIES IN THE LIFE OF LORENZO DE' MEDICI

The women in Lorenzo's life? The count is soon done: two Lucrezias and one Clarice. Lucrezia Tornabuoni, his mother, Clarice Orsini, his wife and Lucrezia Donati, his mistress (Bartolommea Masi, as we shall see, was more of a caprice than true love.) But are they not too few for a man whom Niccolò Machiavelli described as "amazingly involved in sensual affairs" and whom Francesco Guicciardini defined as "licentious and very amorous"?

"Wealth and health - half of half of them" an Italian proverb reminds us. And in the same way, it is as well to calculate half of the half of the ladyloves attributed to many of history's best-known personalities, who, apart from anything else, are not in a position to give themselves up freely to the delights of love.

In the notes to his poetry (almost all of which conventionally speaks of love), Lorenzo makes a confession which, to all intents and purposes, is sincere: "I confess that I am one of those who have loved with great frequency. However, as a lover, I had good reason to doubt rather than trust. Added to this is the fact that, even though more honour and rank has come my way than I deserved, I have, throughout my life, experienced rare pleasures and seen few things worthy of desire. I refer to those things that our soul allows us as relief from public and private labours and dangers."

More than have confidence in women, therefore, he mistrusted them. And they were more of an encumbrance and danger than pleasure, considering his position in society.

He poured his heart into his poetry (love poetry as was the humanistic tradition), whilst his notoriety as a pleasure-seeker gave rise to the interpretation of a business letter commanding "Send fifty skins, all of them from Slavonia" as an order to the Seigneur of Florence to "Send fifty beautiful Turkish slaves".

Lorenzo certainly was not handsome and perhaps it was his faunlike profile which was partly responsible for his renown as a great lover. Vasari tells us that he was short of sight, had a sunken nose and was completely devoid of a sense of smell. He always seemed to be rasping on account of the narrowness of his nose.

Short-sighted, hoarse, with a poor sense of smell. Lucrezia Tornabuoni was the one to donate these physical gifts to her son. The literati of the time called her "ancient" and not "pulchritudinous". She was also short-sighted, with a sunken nose, a high-pitched voice and a poor sense of smell, but otherwise she was a woman of elevated spiritual and intellectual qualities, the worthy wife of Piero the Gouty, unsound of body, but utterly sane mentally and staunch of heart.

Intellectual as she was, Lucrezia Tornabuoni was also an excellent housewife, as can be seen from the letters that she wrote to her family: "I am sending you sixteen flasks of excellent Greek wine, eight flasks of Poggibonsi labelled in ink and eight flasks from Colle". "We find it all good". She ran the housekeeping, saving on everything, even on pigeon chicks: "There are twenty pairs of fledgling pigeons left here," she wrote to her mother-in-law from the villa at Cafaggiolo. "It would be a good idea if you could sell them off in Florence, because here they would just cover expenses without any profit."

She was not miserly, however, and willingly sent presents, just as willingly as she received them. "Oranges, biscuits and fish would be greeted with standards flying". She looked after her children personally and gave news of them to her sick husband: "I wrote to you yesterday that the change suggested by *maestro* Mariotto [the doctor whom she considered to be less competent than she herself was] seemed superfluous to me as Giuliano was better. Last night I noticed that his fever had returned to its previous level".

She also saw to their cultural education, always keeping her husband informed: "Lorenzo is well and, though you are far away, he is always thinking of you. We are getting on well with Ovid, and Giuliano has read four books of history and fables".

Her father-in-law, Cosimo the Elder, reputed her as "the only man in the family" and in Florence they called her the "refuge of all the needy". When she died in 1482, her son Lorenzo wrote to Eleonora d'Este, "I am in despair, as I have not only lost my mother, but my only refuge from many of my troubles and my relief in much toil". And excruciatingly he remarked, "My heart breaks at the mere memory of her!".

When the moment came, Lucrezia Tornabuoni set about finding her son a beautiful and worthy wife who would, above all, be healthy enough to perpetuate the species and, more importantly, ensure the future of the Medici family.

The Florentine damsels were pretty, sprightly and elegant, but they did not come up to scratch as far as their health was concerned. In order to lighten their hair, they would spend hours and hours on the roof tops under the burning rays of the sun, with the result that, as Franco Sacchetti wrote, " they caught their deaths of catarrh".

Dressed in low-necks and dancing away frenetically, they would fall prey to fulminating pneumonia, which was what happened to the beautiful

Among the few extant pictures of Lucrezia Tornabuoni, this youthful one of her is attributed to Domenico Ghirlandaio (Washington National Gallery).

Simonetta Vespucci, the mistress of Lucrezia's other son Giuliano, later to be assassinated.

Piero the Gouty's worthy wife was worried that, on the physical side, she, neither, had brought improvements to the Medici lineage. She looked around her and, not finding anyone in Florence who showed signs of becoming not just a good wife but also (particularly so) a good mother, she set off for Rome on her quest for a daughter-in-law.

Letters have been handed down in which she informs her husband of her search: witty letters, abounding in humour, which were also full of wisdom and, above all, common sense.

After a rather fruitless search, the figure of a sturdy maiden from the noble and powerful Orsini family materialised over the Roman horizon. Lucrezia wrote to her husband, "On Thursday morning, on my way to St Peter's, I chanced to meet Maddalena Orsini, the Cardinal's sister, who was with her daughter of fifteen, going on sixteen". That was just the right age and Lucrezia began to undress the young Orsini girl with her short-sighted eyes, more interested in her physical qualities than in her intellectual ones, as mentioned above.

"She was dressed in the Roman fashion in a *lenzuolo* [a kind of shawl], and she seemed to be handsome, fair and tall in that attire. But I could not see the girl properly because she was entirely covered up".

So she tried to get a better look at her in her cardinal uncle's home, dressed in her house garments... "Clarice was wearing a straight Roman skirt and no shawl. We conversed at great length. And I scrutinised the girl who, as I said, is extremely tall and fair".

She then went on to a more detailed description: "She is not fair-haired because none of the girls here are, but reddish and she has plenty of it. Her face is rather round, but that does not bother me. Her throat is svelte, as is fitting, and is fairly elegant, though I deem it rather too thin".

Lucrezia lowered her gaze from the girl's face to her bosom, which she hoped would be exuberant: "We could not see her bosom because it is the custom to cover it up entirely," she wrote in disappointment, "but it looks well-shaped".

Compared to the Florentines, Clarice Orsini appeared rather awkward and shy: "She does not carry her head well as our girls do, but she pokes it forward. I think this is because she is shy, as I see no other reason for it".

Her motherly pride made her add, "And, when all is said and done, we rate the girl as being a good ideal out of the common, but she cannot be compared to Maria, Lucrezia and Bianca" (her own daughters).

Finally, with a mother-in-law's presumption she remarked, "She is very modest and will soon become accustomed to our customs". Which did not actually happen, because Clarice Orsini kept her coarse and unwavering Roman character. *Vultui suavis, aspera manui* was written on a medal, on the back of which Lorenzo's wife was symbolised by a thorny rose: "Mild in aspect, rough to the touch".

Lucrezia wrote to her husband, "Lorenzo has seen her: try to find out from him if he likes her". He liked the look of her and did not worry about any thorns for two reasons. First and foremost because he would not have touched her all that much and also because he felt he had quite a tough skin. Perhaps he also, like his mother, was only thinking of any children. He accepted their engagement, without concerning himself too much about the Roman maiden, who was in apprehension for the next tournament in which Lorenzo was to take part, but wearing the favour of the other Lucrezia.

Then he wrote in his diary, "I, Lorenzo, have taken *Donna* Clarice, daughter of Signor Jacobo Orsini, as my wife, or rather, she was given to me". The final phrase reveals Lorenzo's feelings when in 1468, at the age of nineteen, he married Clarice who was eighteen. She bore him eight children before dying at only thirty-eight of (incredibly) consumption. It was not a very happy marriage, mostly because Lorenzo did not have the serious character of his father Piero, and Clarice did not have the intelligence of her mother-in-law Lucrezia.

Florence's seigneur kept her confined to their villa at Cafaggiolo in the Mugello Valley almost the whole time. He rarely went there, not caring too much for the hunt. It was his wife who sent him game for the dinners at Via Larga - "I am sending you seventeen partridges, which your falconers caught today".

Certain delicate details disclosed her generous, unselfish nature - "We are all well, thanks be to God. I am sending you a pheasant and a hare because it seems a shame to eat them here just among ourselves". Every day she hoped to see her husband appear, but he always disappointed her, claiming that he had matters of business or government. "I would have so liked you to come and stay here with us, that for three evenings now we have even waited up for you until three o'clock". And in reply to his excuses, she rebutted, "It is hard to believe that your business [in Florence] must needs keep you there". Love *mementoes* thus consisted of hares - "I am sending these two hares, so that in this way you will remember me and the affection I feel for you".

She was not alone at Cafaggiolo. She had her children with her, especially the three boys, Piero, Giovanni and Giuliano, to whom she was not able to give Latin lessons as Lucrezia had. Lorenzo had therefore chosen as his sons' tutor the poet Agnolo Politian, whom Lucrezia Tornabuoni had taken in as an orphan and brought up with her own children. Another poet who was a protégé of Lucrezia was Luigi Pulci.

Clarice, on the other hand, being a religious woman of good sense who was concerned about the moral education of her offspring, preferred the priest, Matteo Franco, who afforded piety as well as culture. Around him was sparked off what can be defined as the war of the poets. Luigi Pulci wrote against Matteo Franco;

Pretaccio da campagna sciagurato
volgiarrosti in cucina e pien di vino
ser Matteo matto tanto avventurato.[1]

And *ser* Matteo complained to Lorenzo, "Gigi is importunate, Gigi is a nuisance, Gigi has a terrible tongue, Gigi is arrogant, Gigi is a scandalmonger. You find a thousand faults in Gigi, and yet nobody can take a breath in your house without Gigi. Gigi is the heart and soul of your guts!".

This latter comment was true with regard to Lucrezia, but certainly not as far as Clarice was concerned as she liked neither Pulci nor Politian. The latter, bored with his life at Cafaggiolo, wrote to his protectress:

"We have been having such a lot of continual rain, that we cannot go out and have abandoned the hunt for ball games, so that the young ones continue to get exercise. I spend my time in a great coat and slippers which, if you could see me, would strike you as so melancholy. I am actually the same as ever and I neither do, see nor hear anything that I enjoy, so distressed am I with thoughts of our calamities which never stop tormenting me whether I am asleep or awake.

The plague and the war occupy my mind the whole time. I have painful memories of the past and I fear for the future. I do not have my lady Lucrezia at my side to whom I might open my heart and I am dying of boredom."

Clarice was right to prefer *ser* Matteo Franco to the two other poets, who were excellent as such, but not as tutors.

The fondness that he felt for Lorenzo and Clarice's sons is revealed in a letter written by *ser* Franco concerning one occasion when Clarice returned from the Val d'Elsa together with Matteo but not with her husband.

Along the road they were greeted with shouts of "*Orso e Palle*" (the Medici arms) and, when they got to Certosa, her three sons, Piero, Giovanni and Giuliano, together with their cousin Giulio, came to meet them. "We met with Paradise full of the angels of revelry and joy" Matteo Franco writes, "that is, Messer Giovanni, Piero, Giuliano and Giulio on horseback. As soon as they saw their mother, they dismounted, on their own or with help and they all ran into their mother's arms and Madonna Clarice, with such glee and

Unfortunately, no portrait of Clarice Orsini painted from true life exists any longer. This eighteenth-century engraving could have been inspired by a portrait extant at that time, or even, quite simply, by a description (Florence, ex Museo Mediceo).

kisses and content that I could not describe it even in a hundred letters". Clarice cannot have been very hard on her children if they greeted her with such an affectionate show of zeal.

Ser Matteo Franco felt affection for those children in the same way and, seeing they were disappointed at the absence of their father, he took Lorenzo's place: "I, myself, could not help dismounting, and before we had put them back in their saddles, I embraced them all and kissed each one twice: one kiss from me and one from Lorenzo".

Their father's absence made the children long for him, as did their mother. "Sweet little Giuliano said, with a drawn-out Oh, 'Ohhhh, where's Lorenzo?' We replied, 'He's gone to Poggio to see you.' He said, almost crying, 'Oh no!' I had never seen anything so touching." It was a pitiful lie that little Giuliano did not fall for and which brought a sob to his throat.

Of anthological worth is the description that the tutor favoured by Clarice gave of the children entrusted to his charge. "There is Piero, who has become a most handsome boy, the most becoming that you have ever seen. He has grown a lot and what a profile he has! His face is angelic, with lovely, rather long hair, much straighter than it used to be, which really becomes him." "And little Giuliano, vivacious and as fresh as a rose, is kind and as clean and bright as a mirror. He is merry, with those eyes lost in dreams." "Master Giovanni, too, looks well, healthy and natural though he has not much colouring." "And Giulio has a good, healthy colour. In a nutshell, they are all joy personified."

Although Giovanni was only nine years old, he was already called "*messere*" because he was destined for an ecclesiastical career. Weak, short-sighted and rather pale, he was to become the first Medici pope under the name of Leo X, whilst his cousin Giulio, with his good, healthy colour, was to become the second, under the name of Clement VII.

It was on account of these two children (and especially the former) that Clarice clashed with the poet Agnolo Politian, who was Lucrezia and Lorenzo's favourite and who would have his pupils read the lascivious Latin poets, while their mother wanted them to read only the Latin of the Psalter, that is, the Psalms as translated by St Jerome.

"As far as Giovanni is concerned," Agnolo Politian wrote to Lorenzo, "his mother keeps him busy reading the Psalter, that I can in no way approve of."

Tension rose to the point that Clarice drove the poet from the Cafaggiolo villa. Politian ran to Lorenzo who offered him hospitality in his residence at Fiesole, almost disavowing his wise wife's conduct. Patiently but firmly, she wrote to him, "Although I have suffered the unpleasant things that were said to me, if it was done with your approval, I will accept it. However, I find it hard to believe".

She felt that she was in the right and the facts confirmed her expectations. Giovanino gave more and more overt signs of piety. He would willingly take communion from the friars at Il Bosco to the amazement of his father and the delight of his mother, who, however, never saw him don his cardinal's hat as did Lorenzo with deep emotion. As we have already mentioned, the wise and attentive Clarice had already died in 1488 at the age of just thirty-eight, yet again a long way from her husband, who was at Bagno di Villa near Lucca where, seriously ill, he was undergoing treatment.

Perhaps Lorenzo felt remorse on that day for having neglected the mother of his children, acknowledging in her that natural wisdom that Lucrezia had divined under the young Orsini girl's shawl.

There was still the other Lucrezia, Lucrezia Donati, whom Lorenzo had met in 1465 when both of them were sixteen.

"He loved a young Donati girl of rare beauty, great honesty and truly noble birth," wrote Niccolò Valori, Lorenzo's first biographer, "in praise of whom Lorenzo not only [wrote] extremely elegant verses and rhymes in the Tuscan dialect, but he also staged entertainments of great magnificence, amongst which was a tournament".

So why was he never betrothed to her? Nothing could stand in the way of a marriage into an even more ancient family than the Medici one. As far as health was concerned, while Clarice Orsini died at thirty-eight, Lucrezia Donati reached fifty-two, outliving Lorenzo himself by nine years.

A strange love Lorenzo felt for this Lucrezia! On reading what the Florentine seigneur wrote about her in presenting his poetry, one might say that it was exclusively literary and poetic.

After the death of the famous Simonetta Cattaneo, loved not by him, but by his brother Giuliano, "I began," wrote Lorenzo, "to try to call to mind whether there was anyone else in our city worthy of such honour, love and praise. I spent quite some time, ever searching and not finding a person who, to my judgement, was worthy of such true and constant love".

But, at last, the figure of Lucrezia Donati advanced. "Among all women, she was one of great beauty to my eyes and of such sweet and charming countenance that, on seeing her, I began to say, 'If this woman has that delicacy, wit and manner that pertained to the dead one, it is certain that both her beauty and grace are greater".

The sonnets inspired by Lucrezia Donati were of the usual Petrarchan type:

Tante vaghe bellezze ha in sé raccolto
il gentil viso della donna mia,
ch'ogni nuovo accidente ch'in lui sia
prende da lui bellezza e valor molto.
Se di grata pietà talora è involto,
pietà giammai non fu sì dolce e pia,
se di sdegna arde, tanto bella e ria
e l'ira, ch'Amor trema in quel bel volto.
Pietosa e bella è in essa ogni mestizia;
e se rigano i pianto il vago viso,
dice piangendo Amor: "Quest'è il mio regno".
Ma quando il mondo cieco è fatto degno
che muova quella bocca un soave riso,
conosce allor qual è vera letizia.[2]

Lucrezia was known to be betrothed to Niccolò Ardinghelli, who had, however, been banished from Florence. Indeed, it was Lorenzo who, in 1465, three years before marrying Clarice, made that marriage possible by allowing Ardinghelli to return to Florence for a few days.

Why did he do this? He could quite easily have impeded that union and any intention to take his pleasure from the bride of an outcast would certainly not have done him any honour at all. If his meeting with Lucrezia Donati had taken place after his marriage to Clarice Orsini, it would have been understandable. But, as already mentioned, Lorenzo ran with Lucrezia's favour in his *giostra,* whilst his betrothed, in Rome, trembled for his safety.

Worse was the conduct of Lorenzo's friends, complaisant pimps, who, during his absences, kept him informed about this new bride. In fact, he was in Milan with Francesco Sforza when Ardinghelli married Lucrezia Donati. Braccio Martelli wrote to Lorenzo at that time:

"Although I know, my dear Lorenzo, that narrating what happened after your departure will, on the one hand, give you grief and, indeed, the more so because you were not here, but, on the other hand, wishing to show you that we have done what you requested, indeed even more than you required, I preferred writing you this letter and causing you displeasure than hiding our enjoyment from you. Nothing was missing from its perfection except your presence which is acutely desired by us and by Lucrezia, as well".

The purpose of these noble gentlemen was seemingly to remind the bride of her distant sweetheart. Indeed, "Many a time," Martelli continues, "have I seen her eyes full of longing for you and her concealing her pain under a smile".

What Martelli then goes on to narrate is reminiscent of Boccaccio because, after the wedding, nine young men and nine girls, including the bride, retired to a villa in San Gervasio, "enjoying themselves greatly, for no-one else appeared and there were no flies around the honey," in other words, the women's husbands were not present!

A year later, in March 1466, Sigismondo della Stufa wrote to Lorenzo who was in Rome, telling him that he had met Lucrezia "in Via de' Servi, who appeared to have been to confession and to be contrite for her sins. [She had] no make-up on and you never saw such a beautiful sight, in that black dress and her head veiled. She stepped so lightly that the stones and walls seemed to bow down to her as she passed by". He ended up: "I will say no more so as not to lead you to sin in this Easter period".

Immediately after his wedding, Niccolò Ardinghelli left for the Levant, where he made a lot of money, while Lucrezia remained in Florence.

It is known from the pen of Alessandra Macinghi Strozzi, a very quick-witted woman who was mother to other outlaws, that Lorenzo did his utmost to get Ardinghelli's banishment revoked "as a favour both to his woman and to Niccolò's, so that she would repay him for it". But, would it not have been better for Lorenzo if the husband had stayed away? Was he, perhaps, worried that he would send for his wife?

"His wife is here and she is enjoying herself," wrote Macinghi Strozzi with feminine malice, not removed from a certain jealousy, "She has had a new dress made with but a few pearls on it, though fine, big ones. And, on the third, she gave a ball in the Pope's room in Santa Maria Novella with Lorenzo, son of Piero, seeing to all the arrangements. And he was accompanied by a group of young men dressed in her livery, with flowing, purple gowns embroidered with fine pearls".

And, alluding to Ardinghelli's good fortune, she wrote to her son who was intriguing at court in Naples for his return to Florence, "Perhaps a beautiful wife is of more use than the help of 47". Ferdinando, King of Naples was indicated with the number 47, whilst the beautiful wife could only be Lucrezia Donati, whom everyone recognised as Lorenzo's mistress.

But how was she loved? Platonically? Poetically? Romantically?

When we find out that Clarice was godmother to one of Lucrezia's daughters, it is hard to believe that Lorenzo would have stooped to such improper behaviour, if his relations with Ardinghelli's wife had gone beyond the limit.

Very different was his relationship with Bartolommea Nasi, indicated by Guicciardini as Lorenzo's last mistress. "His last love was Bartolommea Nasi, the wife of Donato Benci. Although she was not shapely, she was courteous and well-mannered and he was so taken with her that one winter when she was in her country villa, he would leave Florence for five or six hours a night with several companions and would go and visit her, leaving at such time in the morning that he would already be back in Florence when daylight came".

As usual, the historian found that behaviour appalling, especially because of the rank and age of the infatuate or 'ensnared' man. "It is absurd to consider that so important a man, with his reputation and judiciousness, should, at the age of forty, be so taken with a woman who was not beautiful and already advanced in years". As if love were not always something rather irrational which pokes fun at the greatness of any personage, as well as his reputation and judiciousness!

With regard to age, Lorenzo was forty and Bartolommea thirty; one could not truthfully say that she was "advanced in years".

Of course, Lorenzo was already very ill and was to die four years later, leaving a footnote to the previously-mentioned confession which contained the following words to comment on the infrequency of his romances, due to too much renown and the excessive toils of his rank, "I am still very happy to be alive and very content with my lot".

PIERO BARGELLINI

---

[1] Wretch of a country priest, always guzzling roast meat and drinking wine in the kitchen, mad ser Matteo, such a hazard.

[2] So much graceful beauty is assembled / in the noble face of my woman, / that each new circumstance arising donates to it beauty and added value. / If sometimes it is enveloped in a sentiment of appreciation, such sentiment was never so sweet and tender, / if burning with disdain, so beautiful and hard is anger / that Love trembles in that lovely face. / In her is any melancholy pitiable and beautiful; / and if tears line her graceful face, / Love cries sobbing "This is my kingdom". / But when the blind world has become righteous enough / to move that mouth in so sweet a smile, / then it meets with true joy.

ELEONORA DE TOLEDO,
DUCHESS OF FLORENCE AND SIENA

Even for the times in which the wedding of Cosimo I to Eleonora took place, it constituted a singular case in the history of the Medici dynasty of a marriage organised mainly for political ends, but which found a different footing (more intimate and lasting) in the reciprocal love of the wedded couple, almost as if it had been a love-match.

In choosing his bride, the young duke gave a first glimpse of his political acumen which characterised his first years at the helm of the government and also of his skill at divining the moral qualities of those he called to his side.

The notables of the monarchic regime had raised him to princedom on 9 January 1537, in a desperate attempt to make up for the sudden blow dealt to the continuity of the recent dynasty by the assassination of Duke Alessandro. The choice of the senators did not fall on Cosimo just because he was closest of kin to the dead man, but also because his inexperience of state affairs and his young age (he had been born on 11 June 1519) seemingly made him easily influenceable by the *Ottimati* of the Medicean party as far as the government of the principate was concerned.

Cosimino (his boyhood name) had always held himself aloof from political affairs and had lived modestly, without a vast income and under his mother's wing for the most part, some way out of Florence in the villa at Trebbio. Maria Salviati had closed herself in with her religious exercises in the memory of her husband and she had tried to keep this only son of hers removed from the immorality and licentiousness which were a feature of Alessandro's court. Besides, the reigning duke had never held in high regard that obscure relation on the brink of poverty who, furthermore, belonged to a cadet branch of the family having several times shown hostility towards their forefathers, even up to the point of becoming *Populares* and striking up a political attitude which opposed the last seigneur.

Young and exuberant, Alessandro had expected numerous offspring from his bride, recently arrived in Florence and, moreover, he had found his friendship with Lorenzino, the other living member of the Medici family, more congenial. What is more, the latter was a companion on his revels and came before Cosimo in the line of succession to the ducal throne which had been established by Charles V.

So it was that, by taking Cosimo from obscurity and fostering his rise to power, Francesco Guicciardini (along with the other more influential senators) had reckoned that he could count on the new prince's gratitude and inexperience. Allowing himself to be misled by appearances and hopes, the pragmatist politician gave himself up to the idea of easily becoming his omnipotent minister and even - why not? - father-in-law to Cosimo.

However, the young man held by all to be unequal to his new tasks had, in a short time, managed to turn the tables in his favour. In keeping his loyalty to Charles V and in leaving the main strongholds of the state in the hands of the Spanish captains, he had shown that he did not intend to shrink from the political commitments that Clement VII and Alessandro had undertaken towards the Hapsburgs and that he accepted Florence's remaining in the sphere of Spanish interests in Italy. A few months after his election, he had triumphed against the *fuorusciti,* Florentine exiles plotting his overthrow, and, indirectly, against the internal and external political forces which supported them, when he defeated their army at Montemurlo and captured the most feared leaders. By gradually removing the notables of the monarchic regime from power, he had also freed himself very quickly of the supervision that they wanted him subject to, and he summoned new men to positions of great responsibility in his service, men who came from subjugated cities or even from other states in the Italian peninsula. Guicciardini himself experienced bitter disillusionment and his definitive elimination from the Florentine political scene.

At the cost of sacrifice and arduous, unnerving negotiation, Cosimo I finally managed in 1543 to achieve independence once more when he obtained the restitution from Charles V of the strongholds held in pledge of his loyalty. With political intelligence, he set about winning the Emperor's trust, even becoming one of the most influential among his counsellors and supporters in Italian affairs. In the scope of these directives, the duke had actually considered marriage as a means of authoritatively interposing himself among the exponents of the imperial party. Shortly after his being raised to the coronet of princedom, he hastened to request the hand of Margaret of Austria, the illegitimate daughter of Charles V and Alessandro's widow. Marrying her would have enabled him to keep control of the Medici possessions that Alessandro had assigned to his bride, as well as bestowing prestige on him. The family estate, already drastically impoverished following the events which befell the Medicis between 1494 and 1530, would have benefited considerably.

The Emperor, however, had different ideas for his bastard daughter. Just as in 1529 he had promised her hand to Clement VII's favourite so as to gain once more the Pope's friendship and bring him onto his side in the

Eleonora as a young woman (Bronzino, Turin, Pinacoteca).

struggle against France, likewise he now set about using her second marriage in 1538 to Ottavio Farnese to create links with Paul III, the new pope. Besides, although Cosimo had become Duke of Florence, he could not, according to court etiquette, be considered a worthy match for an Emperor's daughter, even an illegitimate one.

In any case, choosing from among the women of important Florentine families would have been a delicate business for the young prince. Such marriages could have become the pretext for rivalry and would have made new enemies for his recent dynasty. Furthermore, marrying a descendant of the Florentine aristocracy was no longer consistent with Medici dynasty directives. For some time now, Medici nuptial alliances tended to underline the distance that had been created between the city lords and the other citizens, however close their ties with the Medicean regime.

Lorenzo the Magnificent had married (1469) Clarice, an Orsini, and in so doing had broken his forefathers' tradition for local brides. He had also married off his eldest son, Piero, to another descendant of that august Roman feudal clan, Alfonsina (1488). Far are we from the sense of moderation in this sphere that had inspired Cosimo the Elder's conduct, who, though omnipotent dominator of Florentine political life, had not forgotten the advantages of keeping up family bonds with the most important families in the city.

In times to come, even after the debacle of the *Signoria* and the decline of the economic fortunes of the family, the skill of Cardinal Giovanni (later Leo X) and the tenacity of Alfonsina Orsini managed to continue this policy which could well be said to have become a dynastic directive.

Close bonds were established with members of other aristocratic families, both Italian and foreign, by means of other weddings. Indeed, in 1515, Giuliano Duke of Nemours had married Princess Philiberte of Savoy and three years later Lorenzo Duke of Urbino was joined in matrimony with Madeleine de la Tour d'Auvergne.

Then came the time in 1529 that Clement VII did not manage to achieve kinship with the House of Hapsburg, although it would only have been through a marriage with Charles V's natural daughter and not with an imperial princess. Political calculation and awareness of dynastic traditions guided the steps taken by Cosimo I in the nuptial field after Charles V's rebuff. The duke turned to Don Pedro de Toledo, viceroy of Naples and, therefore, a leading member of the Spanish nobility, related to the reigning family. A bond with the Toledo family also meant accepting the idea of Spanish predominance over Italy without reserve, as they supported it, together with the Albas, Gonzagas and Avalos, high-ranking bureaucrats or generals of the Emperor and his representatives in the peninsula.

Don Pedro had many offspring, born to his first wife, Donna Maria Pimentel, Marquise of Villafranca. There were as many as four girls; Isabel, Eleonora, Juana and Ana. Cosimo had had the opportunity of meeting them in 1535 on the occasion of his visit to Naples as part of Alessandro's retinue when the latter had to appear before the court of Charles V to defend himself from the accusations of exiles.

Following the custom of the time, the viceroy would have preferred to concede the hand of his eldest daughter, who had rather ugly features. But Cosimo insisted, successfully, on taking the second one, Eleonora, as his wife. She was the prettiest and he had noted her regal bearing and good looks. After winning her hand, he married her by proxy in Naples on 29 January 1538, and received her ceremoniously in Florence the following 29 June.

Accustomed as she was to the splendour of the residence of the viceroy and the ample, princely resources of her family, the young duchess (she had been born in 1522) had at first to adapt to the straightened circumstances of the home in Via Larga where, to make matters worse, continual pillaging and confiscation had dispersed even the artistic heritage which had made it a splendid abode at the times of the Magnificent, an example to the courts of Italy and Europe.

In those rooms, Cosimo had created a work place rather than a princely "court". He did not hold parties, but preferred to live simply, only receiving collaborators in his political and administrative activities, or his intimate friends. It was not that he disdained recreation. Indeed, he loved hunting, horse riding, swimming and fencing and he practised any other type of exercise appropriate for working off the physical exuberance he had inherited from his father. But, most of all, he wanted to dedicate himself to affairs of state and to the administration of the family estate which, at the death of the other Medicis, was all concentrated into his hands.

He intended to reassemble and increase these family possessions. Throughout his life he augmented them with purchases and exchanges, investing great sums of money in the reclamation of waste land, trading with the ships he owned, making loans for interest, buying jewels, building villas - mansions in the city and houses on his country estates. But above all, he resolved to direct all his affairs of state personally. He subordinated the activity of collaborators (who were in truth very capable and had been chosen with intelligence) strictly to his decisions; such men were jurists and politicians, men at arms and ambassadors, administrators and bureaucrats. He also took to heart the problems of guaranteeing justice for all his subjects, of setting to rights the economy of subjected cities, and of ensuring orderly administration in every field, even if that meant subduing the traditional benefits of those "privileged" citizens who had constituted the core of the ruling class under the Republic.

Historians of the principate have perused these aspects of Cosimo's life with particular attention, studying the results obtained: by his policies in the restoration of order; in eliminating the strident differences between Florence and her dominion which had been created and exacerbated by the republican regime; and in enforcing the principle of a juridical system which was inflexible, without any distinction according to wealth or social position. In 1561, Vincenzo Fedeli, a well-informed contemporary who was the Venetian ambassador, delivered his report before the Senate at the conclusion of his mission, thus bequeathing us a lively page on the personality of this prince which is the source of recent historiographical conclusions. Although already well-known, his penetrating judgement on Cosimo's government, is worth relating here. "This prince," Fedeli writes, "governs his dominions with great rigour and dread. He desires the peace, union and tranquillity of his people, who do not dare to make any move. He will not hear any more talk of hate, insult, hostility and vengeance, nor does he wish to hear nominated the Guelph faction or the Ghibelline faction, the Panciatichi family or the Cancellieri, the *Piagnoni* or the *Arrabbiati* [followers and opposers of Savonarola] though all these parties are full of poison for each other. His justice is so equitable, so great and unbounded and so speedy and impartial that everybody keeps within their own confines. He takes great care that disorder should not beak out and nobody should be wronged or treated unjustly and likewise that everybody be punished for their errors regardless of who they are. Finally, with concord between his people and prosperity, peace and justice, the repute of the principate has increased. Neither is there anything lacking, every care and attention being paid that the officials in the regiments and governments are unfailingly skilled men, experienced and intelligent, and just and loyal, above all. And should he discover any malefactor or factionalist, he dismisses him and punishes him indiscriminately … so that civil and criminal disputes are speedily conducted and dealt with."

The portrait sketched by Fedeli is one of a man who is already expert and of a prince who is in control of all state political and administrative reins. But these fundamental aspects of the character of this member of the Medici had already been revealed in the first and toughest years of his rule. The moral qualities of the man must be set alongside with the characteristics of his political persona. Cosimo I did not lead a libertine life. We know of only one love affair during his youth, the outcome of which was a daughter called Bia. He loved her tenderly and took great care of her even after his marriage. But then he became the faithful husband of Eleonora and it was only after her

Maria Salviati, widow of Giovanni delle Bande Nere and the mother of Cosimo I (Vasari, Florence, Palazzo Vecchio, Sala di Giovanni delle Bande Nere).

Lucrezia, fifth daughter of Cosimo and Eleonora, who was married to the Duke of Ferrara and who died at just seventeen years of age, perhaps poisoned by her husband in vengeance for having betrayed him (Bronzino, Florence, Pitti Gallery).

death that he let himself indulge in transitory affairs and form new sentimental liaisons.

He had discerned many aspects in the character of the woman he had requested for his wife similar to his own. To go by her contemporaries, Eleonora had an austere bearing, tinged with haughtiness owing to her Spanish upbringing and the customs of her family of origin. She always held herself aloof, not very inclined to familiarity, conscious as she was of her rank and her position at her husband's side. From this point of view, she succeeded in interpreting to the full that role of sovereign, of *padrona*, which Cosimo deemed he and his companion ought to adopt towards their subjects.

The Florentines neither understood nor loved her. Bejewelled and always dressed in sumptuous clothes, they saw her move along the streets, surrounded by her guards and servants, either closed in her carriage or in the litter which she had had built and which was lined in green satin and covered in velvet of the same colour. Neither did they understand her speech very well, because the duchess knew little Italian and preferred to write and speak in Spanish. Moreover, Spaniards were prevalent among her retinue. They stayed with her for a long time and were not at all welcomed by the "great" Florentines. However, Cosimo did not allow them to interfere in any way in affairs of state or in the life at court.

All the same, whoever bothered to consider many other aspects of Eleonora's day would have noted, along with the arrogant airs that the sovereign adopted in public, the more humane and reserved bearing which characterised her life as woman, wife, mother and mistress of the house.

What was widely said in Florence and reported by Fedeli concerning the duke could also apply as far as Eleonora was concerned. According to him, Cosimo managed to "doff" and "don" the duke whenever he pleased, but only with his own kin because he never let himself go with others. This comment gives us insight into two aspects of his personality: the austere, detached sovereign and the man and father, attached to his family and his sober and reserved life.

Eleonora had a good relationship with her mother-in-law. In fact, in the years of her life that remained after her son had become prince, Maria Salviati participated in family life, even looking after her grandchildren when the dukes were away from Florence on their frequent journeys to one city of the dominion or other. The new mistress of the house did not ring great changes in the tenor of the court life where she had alighted. Indeed, she preserved the modest, austere tone that Cosimo liked; as Fedeli said, "in the home [Cosimo] truly did not live as a prince with that affected grandeur that other princes or dukes tend to adopt, but ... as an out-and-out family man, and he would also eat at a moderately-bedecked table, together with his wife and children...".

The duke wanted, above all, to exploit the function of maternity in the woman who corresponded so closely to his ideals. It was not by chance that he chose the significant phrase *Cum pudore laeta fecunditas* as her motto and, for her device, the image of a pewit gathering her young under her wing. But he admired her as a woman, for the beauty of her face and body, her high forehead, her blonde hair and blue eyes, ever taking delight in the way she conducted herself, discreetly but at the same time aware of her condition as sovereign. As a man, Cosimo also found his senses and feelings assuaged by her and he remained pledged to her, constantly faithful. Fedeli also mentioned this comportment, saying that, after becoming prince, he was not known to have ever conversed with any lady except his wife the duchess, an admirable fact this because it was a source of great satisfaction and pleasure for his subjects. Only when Eleonora died did he "cast all respect aside", as Fedeli's successor, Lorenzo Priuli wrote, allowing himself to make "love to many in a manner which was very open, and especially to one of the chief ladies of Florence [here Camilla Martelli is alluded to; the duke subsequently married her in 1567 so as to regularise the union from which a child had been born] ... which greatly astonished everyone". But - if the digression be forgiven - in this case his behaviour was due to erotic impulses owing to the advancement of cerebral sclerosis, the disease which had already taken hold of him in Eleonora's final months and which was then to carry him off in 1574.

The duchess responded to the duke's love with deep affection, which, from the perusal of documents cited by the historian Pieraccini, could almost be said to have been an exaggerated passion. If true sentiment it were not, then at least it was certainly close to it. Many a time, when the secretaries wrote to the duke, they hinted at the sadness Eleonora felt during Cosimo's absences from Florence and at the sudden joy which took hold of her on the arrival of her husband's letters, which she avidly read and re-read. They reported the change in her expression when mention was made of him in her conversation.

The duke also respected her and did not draw back from conferring on her all necessary power to deal with affairs of state during his longer journeys. In order to better define the affectional relationship between the two and the limits encountered in the reason of state, however, it must be said that tenderness and respect did not prevent them from always dealing directly with their collaborators over the more important issues, sending messengers to reach them wherever they were. Besides, the duke's ministers well knew what his wishes were for each item of business, accustomed as they were to discerning his thoughts and desires regarding governmental problems. Indeed, it was not by chance that documentation in the archives contains no reference at all to Eleonora's intervention in business, because no "rescript" issued by her nor any despatch with her signature can be found. The duchess' function at her husband's side was just limited to asking for leniency, favours or clemency on someone's behalf, and, even in this case, she fulfilled Cosimo's ideal, as he would barely have tolerated a wife with a craving to meddle in the delicate sphere of his sovereign duties.

Many children were born to this deep, lasting love. The first, Maria (1540) was followed by Francesco (1541), Isabella (1542), Giovanni (1543), Lucrezia (1545), Petricco (1546), Garçia (1547), Antonio (1548), Ferdinando (1549), Anna (1553) and Pietro (1554). Eleonora, blessed with a healthy constitution, easily supported frequent child bearing, even though she did so with increasing fatigue, but she did not breast-feed her children herself, both because she was taken up with official undertakings and because such was the established custom in noble families. All the same, many clues show us that the duchess kept her children with her and she loved them tenderly. In fact, she died in 1562 probably from the fatigue she endured (with her already being ill) at Giovanni's bedside and from the grief that the tragedy of those days wrought in her when two sons of hers died within a short time of each other and the life of a third, Ferdinando, was in serious danger.

Repeated child bearing, however, must have contributed to the weakening of her health which was, at one time, so strong and flourishing. Eleonora's biological outline and her rapid physical decline were documented by Pieraccini. Round about 1550, the first symptoms of tuberculosis became obvious, undermining her health and then causing her death. All the same, the historian also reports that the duchess exaggerated in her venting of her physical exuberance; frequent journeys accomplished with her husband, riding expeditions, hunting, and trips from one villa to the other and one country estate to the other in order to keep vigil on her own economic interests and those of her husband.

There is clear evidence of her rapid physical decline; apart from archive documentation, there are Bronzino's paintings which portray her at various times. Two, especially, are extremely eloquent. In the first one (preserved in the Uffizi Gallery) she is still beautiful, dressed in the sumptuous gown she was then buried in and in which her body was found still clothed in 1857 when the Medici tombs were opened to enable the inspection of the state of interment. In the second one (preserved in Berlin), the beauty of Eleonora's face has already withered; her features are jaded and there are evident marks of the illness. She also suffered a great deal on account of her children. The first-born did not live very long, dying in 1557 at the early age of seventeen; Lucrezia, who had become Duchess of Ferrara in 1558, died shortly afterwards in 1561 in circumstances which were not very clear (in fact there was talk of her husband having administered poison to her, in his desire to vindicate her infidelity). Another son, Petricco, died only a few months after his birth. The children who outlived her brought her added anxiety, on account of their turbulent characters and the animosity that since an early age had divided them (Francesco and Ferdinando in particular). The misadventures which rained down on some of the others in their mother's lifetime were painful blows to her, as well.

Among the boys, Pietro, the last-born, had a restless, fiery temperament which did not make him much loved by his siblings and which brought out his worst side, led him to conduct a dissolute life and to commit uxoricide in 1576, unjustly punishing his wife (another Eleonora de Toledo) after having driven her to infidelity through his neglect. Francesco, Garçia and Ferdinando were each brought up very differently, depending on their destiny as established by their dynastic standing, and they suffered from their father's severe treatment (though he did love them) and they very often lived separated one from the other. Particularly distressing was the ever-deepening conflict between Francesco, heir to the throne, taciturn and arrogant, who had been brought up at the court of Philip II in the Spanish way, and Ferdinando, who had a vaster culture and political vision and for whom his father, following Giovanni's death, had resolved an ecclesiastical career, procuring his cardinal's hat while still young in 1563.

Tragic was the fate of Isabella, too, their most cultured and intelligent daughter. A lover of music and song, a poetess and an *improvisatrice*, she was given in marriage in 1558 to the dissolute and cruel Paolo Giordano Orsini, Duke of Bracciano, for political gain. Her husband neglected and abused her and she perished tragically in 1576 by his hand, as he required that she be removed from the scene in order to satisfy the ambitions of his lover, Vittoria Accoramboni, who wished to take her place with the rank of duchess.

These are tragedies, the accomplishment or intended preparation of which did not only distress Eleonora, but also contributed to making Cosimo's character even gloomier. They caused the spread of rumours more or less everywhere throughout Italy and Europe which delineated the ducal court as a place full of hate and crime, painting a dismal picture of the ruling family in the thick of dissoluteness and fraternal conflict. A more thorough research, free of historiographic prejudice, long ago refuted many aspects of that hearsay which was kindled by anti-Medici feeling and scandalmongers, but at the same time it pinpointed the psychological and moral consequences on the tranquillity of the reigning family.

However, relations between Eleonora and Cosimo were not affected; in fact, here were further grounds to cement their union. This is demonstrated by the sincere words that the duke wrote - not only officially but also to his closest friends and collaborators - when Eleonora died. Restrained words of resignation, expressing his pining for her and the bitterness he felt for the solitude that he had to bear after the sudden deprival of the close affection that had bolstered him throughout his difficult life.

But it was not only the family bonds and mutual anxieties of the two which had rendered their amorous harmony and their routine of life so solid. They were also united by their concern for the fortunes of their estate and a common passion for business. The remarks of Fedeli (one of the most acute observers of the ducal family) can once more be quoted. "Cosimo can be seen to have no other intent than that of accumulating valuables," writes the Venetian resident, "and all his children are brought up with that idea..., and the duchess, a woman of rare spirit, treads the same path...". Later on, it is still the same ambassador to paint us a vivid picture of Eleonora's business interests, when he refers to her passion for gambling that she engaged in "for recreation", but where she "always wanted to win and she always played for high stakes". Other documents from the archives studied by Pieraccini describe the disappointment that the duchess felt when she lost and how she did not detach herself from the gaming table even to deal with business (that little amount submitted to her attention) which cropped up during her husband's absence.

With regard to Eleonora's economic concerns, we cite here a few conclusions drawn from documents, all but unknown; they show how she systematically occupied herself with the purchase and sale of real estate, with the application and concession of money loans, and with trade in corn and other foodstuffs. Starting with the sums she brought with her in her dowry in 1539 and her private income, she accumulated considerable wealth in a short time in this way. Even this activity is to be considered globally with the business conducted by Cosimo I on an even wider scale. He often used his wife's wealth for his own financial needs and as often helped her with the transactions that she was about to finalise. The fact is indeed noteworthy that, in stipulating contracts, the couple were both careful to specify that purchases, earnings and benefits, whether direct or indirect, were, in the event of their deaths, to remain in the province of the family, denying each other the right to dispose of any acquired assets in favour of persons who were not a spouse or one of their children.

Eleonora turned her attention principally to the purchase of real estate, houses and farm estates, or to the tillage of uncultivated or marsh lands, which, in the hands of her administrators became fertile and were, in turn, sold or leased out. Her consideration shifted (just as Alfonsina Orsini's had done) to land on the Pisan plain at Barbaricina and Campalto which, at that time, had mostly been abandoned, and where she converted numerous holdings to crop cultivation. A financial estimate of this agricultural activity carried out at the end of the seventeenth century under Grand Duke Cosimo III's orders ascertained that the duchess had spent as much as 26,300 *scudi* on the purchase of real estate.

Long leases, which were just as wide-ranging, were of avail to her for the same purpose, that is to widen her concern to the territories of Campiglia, Giuncarico, Massa Marittima, Castiglione della Pescaia and Grosseto. Cosimo I, meanwhile, operated in the same direction in the Chiana valley. Then, in the area around Grosseto, Eleonora purchased the exploitation rights of the Buriano Lake for herself and for her children, sold to her by the city of Siena and for which she also paid the lord of Piombino an annual impost. This purchase set off another profitable activity, that of selling fish from the lake, which was integrated with similar exploitation of the Castiglione Lake.

While she was buying real estate and planting crops over swampy lands, the duchess invested a great deal of money in Florentine, Spanish and Neapolitan government bonds. In Florence she bought many bank deposits to bequeath to churches and lay charities in her will, or else to leave to her husband and children. She bought a lot of *juros* or Spanish annuities, engaging the considerable sum of 50,000 *scudi,* which rendered her an annual income of 3,571. In Naples she purchased large amounts of fiscal revenues from Baron Niccolò Grimaldi and the viceregal government. She received the island of Troia in the Tyrrhenian Sea as a gift from Iacopo VI Appiani (of a noble Pisan family) and many other gifts were given to her by Cosimo (the Marsiliana estate and 100,000 *scudi* of Neapolitan fiscal revenue), though he inserted the precautionary clause that either could only be disposed of for the benefit of their children.

To complete this brief outline, the income from trade in wheat and money lending should be remembered. Cosimo and Eleonora held a few merchant ships as their private property, with which they traded actively, especially in cereals. A great deal of information concerning this trade can be found in the papers in the Medicean archives. For example, the ducal couple earned enormously in 1554 when, once Siena had surrendered, her famished citizens found, ready at the city gates, vast quantities of grain which the duchess had prepared for distribution. Though it is true that much of this grain was offered free of charge to the neediest, it is also true that, with the devastation in the fields around the city, the Sienese were subject to tax towards their grain suppliers for a long time, so considerable earnings were undoubtedly gleaned from that situation.

As far as loans of money were concerned, we learn from the previously-mentioned seventeenth-century financial estimate that, still in collaboration with her husband, Eleonora borrowed as much as 58,000 *scudi* in various stages (Cosimo I handled money in loans for over a million *scudi*). To guarantee repayment, she utilised the annual income received from the duties on salt and flour which constituted her ordinary appanage, or else the government bonds which, as already mentioned, were included in her personal property.

According to her will, written on her death bed in Pisa on 16 December 1562, all Eleonora's belongings passed on to Cosimo I, with the exception of a few bequests in favour of grooms, the ladies of her court who were still unmarried and slave girls who, by the same deed, were declared free.

Even in these circumstances, Eleonora demonstrated that, above all else, she was attentive to her husband and children's well-being. However, her fortunate economic activity would not have been so worthy of note (even though such pursuits were unusual in reigning princesses) if it had not given the Medici and, indirectly, Florence some assets of a high artistic value, casting the foundations for the building of monuments which can still be admired today and which go to make up the historical heritage of the nation of Italy. In fact, it is thanks to Eleonora that Palazzo Pitti was purchased. At the time of their wedding, as already mentioned, Cosimo I's small court still resided in the mansion on the Via Larga. But the growing needs of the family and the explicit political aim to uphold the new principate over memories of the defeated republic soon induced the duke (1540) to move into the so-called palace "in the Piazza", i.e. the official residence that the gonfalonier and the priors had lived in since Dante's times.

He ordered huge works of restoration and adornment of those rooms, getting Vasari to decorate the gonfalonier's apartment which was made over to Eleonora's quarters, and incorporating into the rooms where he held his court other adjoining apartments, such as those of the justice executive (judiciary which had long previously been suppressed) and of the captain of the foot-soldiers. The new ducal guard, made up of Swiss lancers (the "Lanzi") were quartered in barracks in Via Lambertesca and were accommodated on duty in the loggia built by Orcagna which used to belong to the *Priori*.

Another six children were born in the palace "in the Piazza". They lived out their infanthood on the top floor of the new home, playing on the terraces open to the air and sun. But, little by little, this residence, too, turned out to be unsuitable for the requirements of family and court. The workers in the principate's offices needed more and more space and facilities as their duties expanded and room had to be found for them as well within the walls of the same building, so that they could operate near the sovereign who wished to follow their activity closely.

The grand project of urban renewal that Cosimo longed for began to take shape with the purchase of Palazzo Pitti, accomplished gradually (as with so many other Medici enterprises) between 1550 and 1565. With her own money and in full agreement of intent with her husband, for about 9,000 gold florins Eleonora purchased the Boboli Palace in 1550 from members of the Pitti family. At that time it consisted in just the central block with three central arches and the seven windows lying above them. The building went no higher than two floors and, what is more, the roof was missing, as the Pitti family, rich as they were, had not had the means to complete it. Cosimo summoned Ammannati (1560) to draw up the designs and complete it. With a great deal of foresight, Eleonora had also bought up a lot of land round about and a quantity of houses at the sides of the building, with a view to its being enlarged at some future moment. For his part, the duke laid out the gardens with the help of Tribolo and Buontalenti. They were conceived both as a place of recreation for the family and as an area for rest or court ceremony. A painting by Justus Utens represents them as they appeared at the end of the sixteenth century. However, the palace "in the Piazza" was never abandoned as official residence and both palaces were used as places of work and representation. In 1560, in the duchess' final years, he began the construction of Vasari's Uffizi, conceived to hold the most important judicial offices, and he also began to contemplate the idea of connecting the palace "in the Piazza" with the Pitti along a gallery passing through the Uffizi and over the Ponte Vecchio, so that the court residence and the Magistrates' offices would become an organic whole, operating harmoniously around the sovereign. By 1565, the passage had been built on Vasari's project.

Notes on Eleonora's personality would not be complete if mention were not made of her attitudes to religion and charity. The duchess did not display a superior mentality in this field either, limiting herself to punctiliously observing liturgical offices, dispensing charity towards the city's deserving works, hospitals and monasteries.

This, of course, was partly her duty as sovereign. It is a known fact that her name is, for the most part, tied to the foundation of the Jesuit college in Florence which she steadfastly desired on account of her high respect for Father Lainez, the highest-ranking companion of Saint Ignatius Loyola.

Cosimo I did not appear in favour of welcoming the fathers of the Society of Jesus to his capital city (at least not at first), but Ignatius Loyola knew he could count on the duchess backing him up as she wanted Lainez in Florence to hear him preach and to have his spiritual guidance. The first meeting between Eleonora and the Jesuit took place in 1548, after Paul III had allowed Lainez to leave Rome as a favour to the duchess. The father did not make a good impression on her at first, but then, as reported in a chronicle kept among the papers in the Florentine State Archives, Eleonora "heard him speaking in public and was exceedingly impressed". However, St. Ignatio's plan to open a college in Florence was not, for the moment, followed through because of Cosimo's doubts as to whether it were not preferable to open one at Pisa, where he intended to concentrate all centres of study. Loyola, on the other hand, considered the presence of his order more useful and significant in the cradle of humanistic culture.

Other circumstances favourable to Ignatio's project were created between 1548 and 1551 with the declared wishes of the Cathedral canons, together with a few gentlemen, to accommodate in Florence the "Reformed Fathers" who were bringing so much spiritual benefit to other important cities throughout the peninsula. In 1551, Lainez tried again and sent the duke a memorandum, remarking on the spiritual advantages which he considered would be the outcome of founding a college in Florence and also listing the places in Italy and elsewhere to which the Jesuits had been welcomed with open arms by their princes and people. Not least among those cited were those places under the dominion of Spain, where the representatives of the Catholic king and the aristocracy had fallen over themselves to welcome the religious order and aid them with generous donations. The appeal did not go unheeded. Political expediency, pressure from the duchess and also, perhaps, the sincere desire to facilitate the renewal of the city's religious customs in some way induced Cosimo I to accommodate them. So it was that the Jesuits opened their first home in the San Frediano quarter in 1551 until they could move to the church and parochial building of San Giovannino in 1554 after also having lived elsewhere.

We have also mentioned the duchess' charity work and the gifts that she bestowed on monastic foundations, falling into line with the practice of the time and the prevailing custom of the reigning Florentine family. In this respect, it is of interest to remember how, with papal brief on 1 January 1561, Pope Paul IV granted her a legal reserve of income from benefices with the undertaking to invest it in work for charity. With the Pope's consent, Eleonora earmarked the vast sums which would be made available for the construction of a convent for the wives and daughters of the Knights of Santo

Stefano, the military order that the duke founded in 1562. However, her untimely death did not permit her to carry out that intention, subsequently taken up and completed by her husband and sons, Francesco and Ferdinando, using the legacies left in her will. The three grand dukes constructed the so-called "new Convent of the *Concezione*" in Via della Scala, the walls of which are still standing today, though the building was turned to different use after the convent was suppressed in 1864.

Many times in the course of this rapid biographical review have we referred to the dramatic circumstances of Eleonora's death. This came about owing to a fatal succession in natural events. As had happened other times previously when Cosimo had had to inspect fortifications in the Maremma, Leghorn and Pisa, he requested that his wife accompany him. It was thought that the trip to the milder climates of the places where the ducal couple were to visit would have done her good; the pulmonary haemorrhages which tormented her had become frequent and copious. Their sons Giovanni, Ferdinando and Garçia wished to go along with their parents for a change and a little enjoyment, though the doctors had warned of the risk of contracting the malaria which in those months infested the Maremma district. Fate proved the doctors to be right. The three princes fell ill. Giovanni and Garçia died at a short time of each other and their mother followed them to her tomb three weeks later. Ferdinando struggled against death at length. These are the basic facts of the drama that, in just a few days, carried away from Cosimo I his most promising and most dear which were his wife and sons, Giovanni especially, for whom he intended to pave the way to the papal throne.

But, as we have said, political hatred and gossip took advantage of the opportunity for substantiating the legend of a domestic tragedy which spread from Rome to Venice, to France and to Trento, where the bishops were assembled in council. It was said that, during a hunting party, the princes had had an argument, in the course of which Garçia had stabbed Giovanni; shortly afterwards, an irate Cosimo had run the survivor through when he had come begging his mother's forgiveness; overcome with grief she herself died a few days later.

The rumour itself has its own story which a Medicean scholar, Saltini, pieced together at the end of the nineteenth century, demonstrating it to be groundless. The letters that Cosimo wrote in the days of the tragedy to his son Francesco in Spain are still kept in the State Archives. We learn from these letters that, on 15 November, Giovanni (together with his brothers) fell ill with a 'malignant fever' and died five days later, when the duke informed his distant son that the party would have moved onto the cleaner air of Pisa. But on 18 December, he wrote again to say that Garçia had got worse and had died on the twelfth day of the month and that the duchess, worn out with caring for her sick sons, had passed away six days later. The details of the events gleaned from these letters are strongly convincing, but for centuries after, just as strong were the effects of the scant sympathy borne by Florentine historians towards the Medici, on whom the accusation of having effaced freedom was constantly hung. So it was that, many a time between the seventeenth and nineteenth centuries, the legend formed the basis for erroneous and tendentious conclusions. As has already been mentioned, it was only later on, in a more relaxed and critically-founded historiographic climate, that the true facts were recognised.

But, for the people involved, the true facts were no less dramatic and painful. The events of 1562 marked a definite turning point in the personal story of the man Cosimo, even though they did not distract him from the tasks he had taken upon himself on behalf of the state. No longer buoyed up by the tacit moral support of the woman who had loved and understood him, the duke became gloomier and more reclusive, and began to take his distance from the family who, regardless, surrounded him with a jealous, possessive love.

At his side, Eleonora had been an adoring and ever-faithful wife, a sovereign and a mistress of the house, a companion in whom he could confide projects and hopes, together building up their political and economic future. Above all, with reciprocal affection the couple had managed to substantiate a long-lasting marriage which had been born out of dynastic interests, not love.

To round off the biographical essay of this Spanish woman who had come to Florence in one of the most dramatic periods of the city's history, when secular freedom gave way to subjection, I wish to recall the positive aspects of her personality, the intimate aspects of her character and the fact that she was at the side of a prince who, in the shadows and the glitter of his political enterprises, remains one of the most significant figures of the Italian Cinquecento.

ARNALDO D'ADDARIO

BIANCA CAPPELLO

First rejected and persecuted by her family, then declared "dearly beloved daughter of the Venetian Republic", Bianca Cappello moved on from the role of more or less secret mistress to that of grand duchess of Tuscany. She never received good reports from the chronicles of the time; indeed, an unshakeable, pitiless tradition pursued her in life and in death, pointing her out as a dangerous sorceress who was also gifted with the mysterious intermediary powers of a medium, colouring her every action black and holding her responsible for misdeeds she did not perpetrate. She was certainly not a woman of heroic virtue, quite the opposite. She was always weak and often guilty, but she was also endowed with humane qualities and I believe she deserved a trial of appeal that was not at hand for her, with scarcely documented eulogistic writings harming more than benefiting her.

Bianca was little more than sixteen years old on the night between 28 and 29 November 1563 when, engulfed in a cloak, she slipped silently out through a back door of the austere Palazzo Cappello on the side giving onto the Salviati bank, where a young man, Piero Bonaventuri, was waiting for her. They both headed for the quay, escorted by his old uncle, Giovan Battista, in trepidation, though delighted, for his nephew's wild escapade, and Bianca's ever-present nurse, devoted, impassioned and ambiguous, such as befitted the figure of the nurse which through history, art and legend has been handed down to us (today definitely vanished from our lives and literature in virtue of the freer and easier ways of our times). It was a dark, foggy night, with the swash of the high water covering every sound of the oars. The couple managed to reach dry land by gondola and begin their none too easy journey towards Florence.

That had not been Bianca's first clandestine outing; in fact it was the culmination of a long spell of flirting with the Bonaventuri youth who, she had at the beginning been led to believe (indeed as he pretended with his carefree Venetian company), was the son of the banking family Salviati. In actual fact, he was a member of the family of Salviati's agent, sent to Venice to learn how to deal in business and to find decent employment. He found Bianca, instead, a lovely little blonde from a patrician Venetian family, great granddaughter of Elisabetta Cornaro, related on her father's side to the descendants of Vettor Pisani and on her mother's to the Morosini.

Bianca's mother, the beautiful Pellegrina Morosini, had died when the child was just twelve. In dying, she left her own dowry for her, plus all her jewels. The Cappello family never paid Bianca those dowries, neither when they were offended (rightly so) with the Bonaventuri, nor when they were proud of seeing her, "dearly beloved daughter of the Venetian Republic", seated on the grand ducal throne. The gems that the damsel took with her when she eloped constituted a charge against her, and, let it be said in passing, not the least substantial one at that.

Left on his own, Bartolomeo Cappello mourned his wife intensely, even though briefly so because, at less than a year of her death, he was already re-married to Lucrezia Grimani, the widow of Andrea Contarini, with doges for grandparents and the prince-patriarch of Aquileia for a brother. The new mother interpreted her mission by setting the girl apart in a wing of the mansion and restricting her outings to what was indispensable for her to fulfil her religious duties and to appear in the bosom of the family on official occasions. Perhaps she took fright at her step-daughter's temperament or she was jealous of her beauty which became more and more evident with each day that passed and which, among her many virtues, she did not possess.

What can a restless child do, confined indoors and isolated between her crocheting and the harpsichord, except gaze out from the balcony and become enchanted by the glances of this handsome lad, just as, later, it was his easy Florentine parlance to enchant her? The course of events suggested flight, seeing as there was no chance that a pretender of scarce nobility and even less wealth could be welcomed into such a gathering of high society. Perhaps the suspicion of approaching motherhood hastened along the unfolding of events, because the couple took flight by land and sea at the end of November and their daughter, Pellegrina (Bianca wanted her named after her own mother), was born on 23 July 1564, after the couple, offered refuge by the Bonaventuras out of a mixture of dismay and kindness, had been secretly married in the church of St Mark's.

Secretly, because the Cappellos, highly offended, were eager to avenge the two lovers. Their own honour was at stake, as was that of the Morosini, the Grimani, Vettor Pisani's heirs and the whole Venetian participate. Their immediate reprisal was to imprison Bianca's nurse and uncle and, despite the protests of the Salviati family and even the Medici, they did not liberate the old man even when he was dying of heart trouble. At the same time, they offered a reward of exceptional size on the head of the wretched kidnapper, so the young couple were reduced to living barricaded in their lodgings, in constant danger of being killed by cut-throats hired to reconstruct the family honour by carrying out their vengeance.

Bianca thus went from one prison to another. The second one in St Mark's Square was decidedly less gilded than the one in the Cappello

This portrait of Joanna of Austria with her son Filippino shows us Francesco I's wife (defined by a contemporary as "ugly, cold and a hunchback") shows quite a pleasant aspect. Credit is perhaps due to Bizzelli who tried to beautify the grand duchess (Florence, Uffizi Gallery).

mansion on account of her mother-in-law's miserliness and their economic restraints, though the Bonaventuras were not in real poverty. And from what can be gathered, fate would have it that a side-window came into play here, as well. If the truth were told, Francesco, first-born of Cosimo I and Eleonora de Toledo, was not struck by Bianca's beauty when he caught sight of her through the window, but rather it was the couple who entrusted themselves on the prince by means of intermediaries, begging him to intercede with the Cappello family and to bestow his protection on them ... and they got much more than they had bargained for.

Francesco was twenty-three when, in 1564, his father had off-loaded onto him the weight of governing the grand duchy with the title and attributions of regent. He had been handed the government of a unitary state which his father had formed by overcoming the obstacle of the communes' self-government, a state enlarged with the subjugation of Siena, which provided an outlet to the sea in the port of Livorno (subsequently realised in full by Francesco and Ferdinando). It was also a state with an army, a fleet and a growing capital city constantly enriched in the intellectualistic climate of mannerism (suffice it to consider the building of the Uffizi, begun by Vasari in 1560 and already at an advanced stage, which constituted an audacious perspective opening within the bounds of the Mediaeval cities). A state, let it be said, which was basically strong, but burdened with the categorical imperative of having to steer a middle course in a subtle game with the great powers and having to rise above the rivalry of other Italian states.

Knowing how authoritarian Cosimo was and how intensely, almost joyfully, engrossed he was in his sagacious art of government, it is difficult to find an explanation of this renunciative attitude of his. One is tempted to think that he wished to retire from the political scene where he had played a leading role, so as to foster his son's elevation to the rank of grand duke. But it has to be admitted that a sense of fatigue probably contributed to his decision, as if he had had a foreboding of precocious ageing (despite his only being forty-five), and that he felt consternation for that mysterious nemesis that had wiped out his family in such a brief space of time.

Perhaps there were a series of reasons which persuaded him to hand over the command of the state to his son, keeping the title and supreme authority for himself and retiring to private life, comforted by Eleonora degli Albizi - he who had been so faithful to his wife while alive - and then by Cammilla Martelli.

Francesco willingly took the weight of government upon himself, bolstered by the pleasure of commanding and by his burning ambition, which, after all, was to lead him to accept (without excessive enthusiasm, but

Few are the portraits which can be said to represent Bianca Cappello with certainty. This portrait, as well, is only by tradition considered to represent her (School of Bronzino, Florence, Pitti Gallery).

without resentment either) the contrived marriage with Joanna of Austria, daughter of Emperor Ferdinand I, sister of Maximilian II and niece of Charles V. The wedding was celebrated in the Santa Maria del Fiore Cathedral in Florence on 18 December 1565 with a stately scenographic array and manifold festivities, under the direction of Vasari, Borghini and Caccini.

The royal bride was certainly blessed with many virtues: she was austere, pious and determined to be a good wife and mother (which, in fact, she was). But these were not endowments which by themselves could enchant the heart and senses of a young husband such as Francesco and keep him from turning for the worse, dragged down by his love for Bianca.

At seventeen, Joanna appeared to the chroniclers of the time to be rather humped and not beautiful. Some even wrote that she "was ugly, cold and a hunchback" and her portraits seem to confirm this, with her long, wan face, protruding nose and lips and vacant gaze. Furthermore, perhaps intimidated by her new surroundings, she was incapable of communicating because of difficulties with the language which she never managed to master. She did not possess the gift of congeniality, remaining extraneous and hostile to family and court circles, extraneous to the city that had welcomed her with such enthusiastic joy and extraneous to the culture, traditions and blossoming artistic wealth of her new country.

In her honour and so as to put some life into her entry into Florence, the city had quite literally got dressed up in its finery: the fountain glistening in the main square with Ammannati's Neptune in the centre made a beautiful effect, the only authentic piece in a (then) only temporary setting (although the Florentines had immediately baptised it "i' Biancone" (The White One), chanting "O Ammannato, O Ammannato, / quanto marmo tu ha' sciupato[1] ...". The Cathedral had been white-washed to welcome the bridal couple and was resplendent in its new-found dichromatism. Then, in Palazzo Vecchio, besides Eleonora's apartments, the courtyard had been renovated with Michelozzi's great pillars embellished with stucco grotesques on a gold background and panoramic views of Austrian cities painted on the walls.

Joanna, however, instinctively perceived the superficiality of such a display, which did not manage to thaw her coldness, or perhaps it was shyness. Worse was to follow when, made aware of the relationship between her husband and Bianca Cappello through the good offices of a lady in the court, she became jealous, complaining and moaning, erratically disposed towards her rival, now heaping kindness on her, now treating her with express disdain. Though she had all the justification in the world, she became the worst thing a woman can become ... a nagging wife. In contrast, Bianca became still more beautiful, affable and tender, now that motherhood had

The approval of the Franciscan order - portrait of Lorenzo the Magnificent (D. Ghirlandaio, Florence, Basilica of S. Trinità).

The so-called "Dama del Mazzolino" by Verrocchio is generally considered to be a portrait of Lucrezia Donati (Florence, National Museum of the Bargello).

Lorenzo the Magnificent (C.16th Florentine School, Florence, Palazzo Medici Ricciardi).

Leo X (Raphael, Florence, Uffizi Gallery).

In this charming portrait by Bronzino, Eleonora is represented in the maturity of her beauty. Her fourth child, Giovanni, stands beside her. He was to die at nineteen years of age, a few days before Eleonora herself (Florence, Uffizi Gallery).

Portrait of Cosimo I in armour (Agnolo Bronzino).

Maria, the firstborn of Cosimo and Eleonora, is portrayed in this delightful portrait painted by Bronzino (Florence, Uffizi Gallery).

Garçia, seventh child of Cosimo and Eleonora, who died when fifteen at the same time as his brother Giovanni and his mother (Bronzino, Florence, Uffizi Gallery).

Charles V (Antonio Van Dyck, Florence, Uffizi Gallery).

One of the supposed portraits of Bianca Cappello, though this opinion is not supported by documentation (Alessandro Allori, Florence, Uffizi Gallery).

Portrait of Madame Christine of Lorraine, widow of Ferdinando I de' Medici (Florence, Uffizi Gallery).

Catherine de' Medici, Queen of France, in a portrait by François Clouet (Florence, Pitti Gallery).

Marie de' Medici, Queen of France, in a portrait by Pulzone (Florence, Pitti Gallery).

Justus Sustermans, official court painter of the Medici, here portrayed Vittoria Della Rovere in the pose of the vestal virgin Tuccia, a mythical virgin who, on being unjustly accused, succeeded in proving her innocence by carrying water in a sieve (Florence, Pitti Gallery).

An official portrait of Marguerite d'Orléans (Unknown painter of C.17th, Florence, Pitti Gallery).

The Elector and Electress Palatine loved entertainments and dances. This painting by van Douven charmingly demonstrates the court life at Düsseldorf and the costumes of the time (Florence, Pitti Gallery).

transformed the attractive young girl into a stunning woman. Even many years later, this beauty, which was indisputable (even though not much in keeping with our present tastes) and despite a premature tendency to plumpness, must still have been more than a shadow of itself when Bianca, Grand Duchess of Tuscany, graciously welcomed a youthful Galileo Galilei who had asked her for a letter of recommendation for the University of Pisa. The young scientist was completely overwhelmed and one of his biographers, the Hungarian Von Harsanyi, romantically attributes the raging passion which bound him to Marina Gamba to the latter's extraordinary likeness to Bianca.

The position of the Bonaventuri couple, by now officially introduced into court circles, acquired increasing importance. Pietro was in charge of His Highness' linen, while Bianca appeared among the palace ladies, though clearly not well-received by Joanna. She made friends with Francesco's very beautiful sister, Isabella Orsini di Bracciano, who already seemed in the eye of an atrocious destiny and who counterpoised the grand, sullen court of Palazzo Vecchio in those years with the more brilliant, open-minded atmosphere, sparkling with culture and good taste, at the Medici home in Via Larga. In the meanwhile, children were born, lots of them ... not to Bianca who was already mortified at the knowledge of not ever being able to give Francesco any children, but to the Prince and Joanna and also to Cosimo and Eleonora degli Albizi - that self-same Giovanni who was to become architect of the *Cappella dei Principi* (Medicean Chapel) - and, a year later, yet again to Cosimo, this time by Cammilla Martelli.

The grand duke's leisure was quite obviously fecund! But when, after the birth of Virginia, the private citizen Cosimo wanted to marry Camilla, "a decent, Florentine gentlewoman and *bona figliola*" - how racily Tuscan that *bona figliola* is - he met with the most relentless hostility in his sons Francesco, Cardinal Ferdinando and Piero, who for once all agreed in their feeling peeved and offended, together with the haughty animosity of his daughter-in-law who ran in protest to her imperial relations.

The grand duke forcefully put her in her place saying to her, "I tell you, my lady, that I seek no quarrels, but I will not shun them if they are forced on me in my own house". This was perhaps his only forceful deed against his daughter-in-law, while he never grew tired of trying to intervene affectionately and make peace between husband and wife. "The Prince is very fond of you", he wrote to her, beseeching her to make it up with her husband and "to suffer youth to have its fling, and to endure with patience that which time will shortly remedy". Each time Joanna willingly consented to make peace and each time the outcome was a child, a daughter, in fact, because only in 1577 did the longed-for male heir, Prince Filippo, come into the world, only to close his brief life on earth in 1582.

By this time, Bianca and her husband were living in the Via Maggio mansion, renovated for them by Buontalenti and decorated with graffito work by Poccetti. They alternated staying in this sumptuous city residence with spells at the splendid Villa della Tana at Sant'Andrea a Candeli, just outside Florence. Pietro took advantage of his position at court to the extent that he abused it, thus rousing envy and animosity which increased his wife's discomfort. He pursued reckless, risky adventures. Bianca's behaviour towards her husband and his family was clear to everyone; she must have been almost maternally fond of him because she always defended him and tried to patch up his misdeeds. That is why it would seem unjustifiable to blame her for complicity in his murder on 26 August 1572 by the hand of Roberto Ricci, a relative of Cassandra Bonciani, one of his lovers, who was to suffer the same destiny the following day.

It is certainly not for me to take on Bianca Cappello's defence counsel, but, if I may, I wish to pose the question which lies at the base of any juridical investigation: *cui prodest*? Who would have benefited from the death of this unfortunate man? What obstacle did he represent for the two lovers? With his outlook, he had favoured the bond between the prince and his own wife which had become very close and was flaunted rather too much. And even if he had not gone so far as to throw her into the prince's arms, he had wrung all possible advantages, honour, money and power from the situation. Besides, the eventuality of the grand duchess dying could not be contemplated because she was just twenty-four and that same year had felicitously given birth to her fifth child. Indeed, on a closer look, Bonaventuri represented the last shield of so-called "decency" for his wife, who, once made a widow, was incessantly invited by the Cappello family to return to her homeland. However, she refused on Isabella Orsini's advice, knowing full well that at best she could expect to be shut away in a convent for good. She even took flight in the face of the persistence of Venetian ambassadors who (she feared) were spies of her family, intent on forcing her hand.

Years later, fleetingly overcome by scruples of conscience, the grand duke confessed that he had known what was being plotted against Bonaventuri, but that in no way had he been involved and had left things to go their own way ... which did not redound to his credit either for his moral perception or for his astuteness, because, by leaving events to take their course, suspicion was logically massed against him and his supposed accomplice. In his very clear-cut study on the Prince of the *Studiolo*, Luciano Berti subtly analyses Francesco's character: cultured, romantic, continuing in the most noble family traditions. It would be enough just to consider the phenomenal artistic blossoming of his capital city and, to mention but a few works, the institution of the Uffizi Gallery, Buontalenti's Tribune (containing gems of the Medicean collection) and, above all, the *Studiolo* in Palazzo Vecchio that he wished to have built and decorated as a precious strong box, where he aspired to amalgamating art and craftsmanship in complex symbology. But he was also psychologically inward-looking, inspired and very keen on science, though he tended to transform himself from scientist into alchemist and almost into sorcerer.

That he had a tenacious, idle disposition and was capable of outbursts of generosity and also of savage cruelty is confirmed by his unpardonable behaviour with regard to Camilla Martelli, his father's morganatic wife, whom he had put away in the Convento delle Murate as soon as Cosimo had closed his eyes for the last time on 21 April 1574. At that time it was not a prison (it became so a few centuries later), though it was such for the poor woman who was not even allowed to witness the grand pomp and ceremony of her husband's funeral. He gave proof of his cruelty in his atrocious vendetta not only on the actual conspirators led against him by Orazio Pucci, but also on mere suspects, all of them massacred without mercy. His attitude was ambiguous and inert (though he was resigned at heart) when he endorsed as accidental the death of his sister-in-law, Eleonora, (in actual fact strangled at Cafaggiolo by her husband) and also that of his very dear sister, Isabella Orsini, she, too, murdered by her husband. The two crimes which were committed one after the other in the space of a few days on 9 and 16 July 1576, threw a sinister light over Francesco and the Medicean court, giving rise to discontent in a large section of public opinion, and must have appalled Grand Duchess Joanna who was not at first informed of these goings-on but who, yet again, turned in alarm to her imperial brother.

The victims were both beautiful, cultured and spirited. Eleonora, daughter of don Garçia de Toledo and consequently niece of the other Eleonora, had been brought up at the palace like a daughter. She had married her cousin Piero at the age of eighteen, perhaps in the hope of curbing the youthful unruliness of Cosimo's youngest son, who, for the whole of his unfortunate life seemed to wholly epitomise all the Medici shortcomings without appearing to possess any of their qualities. Apart from the name, Eleonora echoed her aunt's serene beauty and warm, passionate temperament. On being neglected and insulted by her husband, she entered into "close friendship" with a Florentine gentleman with the name of Bernardino Antinori, whom love had turned into a poet, amiable if not gifted. The romance had blossomed amidst the various parties, serenades and balls. It would have been better for Antinori if he had not even sympathised with

Orazio Pucci's conspiracy (though he had not taken part) and had not thus offered a pretext to be thrown into jail and executed on 20 June at the Stinche prison.

When Eleonora was ordered by her husband to join him at the castle of Cafaggiolo, she was seized by the direst foreboding and went with desperation in her heart ... In the evening of the following day, a short procession returned to Florence bringing the coffin where the beautiful creature's body had been hastily recomposed. Piero wrote these exact words to the grand duke, "At six o'clock last night, my wife met her death in an accident. Your Highness should set his heart at rest, however, and write to tell me what I must do". So Francesco endorsed his brother's crime, taking upon himself to illustrate to the Spanish court how his honour had had to be restored. His explanations were apparently accepted as convincing and that was the end of the matter. The strangling of Isabella by her husband at Cerreto Guidi, on the other hand, was the beginning of a tragic "boomerang" which struck back at the murderer himself, Paolo Giordano Orsini, of the very powerful family of Bracciano. Though bound by eighteen years of marriage, the couple lived practically separated. To the princely abodes of her husband, Isabella preferred the freedom of the mansion on Via Larga, of which she was the main ornament. After many stormy liaisons, Orsini had come to a standstill in his almost conjugal love of the very beautiful Vittoria Accoramboni. There was certainly no rekindling of an old flame with regard to his wife, nor was there an outburst of wounded pride (though he did suspect a relationship between Isabella and a nephew of his), but it was probably his desire to marry his lover which induced him to rid himself of his wife.

His brother-in-law's example stimulated him to regularise his aggravating family situation under the guise of washing away the shame of his wife's unfaithfulness. So for Isabella, too, was mention made of an indisposition, of a stroke which hit her while she was washing her hair - forgetting to state the fact that at the time her head was in a noose or "dog's lead", making her face swell up horrifyingly. *Annus horrendus*, if ever there was one, this 1576, when even the state structures seemed to teeter: famine, plagues of locusts of biblical proportions devouring the crops, widespread discontent concerning the burden of taxation, a very high cost of living in Florence, more so than in any other city in Italy, which caused a surge of criminality and banditry.

And to lend the finishing touch, after keeping up a simulation of pregnancy for nine months, Bianca announced that she was now mother to a son, recognised as his by the grand duke who was always to provide generously for him. This is one instance where the ancient saying, *Mater semper certa, pater incertus* can be overturned, because, though the true father may well have been undetermined (it was also said that, to consolidate her position, Bianca passed off as hers the illegitimate son of the grand duke and another woman), there is only one certainty regarding the mother: that she was certainly not Bianca Cappello!

Two years later, in the April of 1578, the grand duchess sustained premature childbirth, following an unfortunate accident. Due to the incapacity of her attendants, her death ensued after a harrowing labour, which is described in detail by historians, but which I shall, of course, pass over. I shall, however, transcribe the death report which strikes me as curious and rather off-hand: "Her spine was twisted into an S ... her liver was hard and bloodless, her lungs inflamed and glued to her breast. Apart from that, she was well". Those were the very words!

The period following her rival's passing away must have been a most distressing and uncertain time for Bianca because, moved by his wife's resigned suffering, her strength of character and her exhortations, the grand duke took his distance from his mistress and put the belated scruples of his conscience before an assembly of confessors and theologians. It was a short-lived crisis, but it revived the hopes of Bianca's enemies, especially those of Cardinal Ferdinando. However, when he had recovered from his predicament, Francesco decided to marry her, which he did, secretly, on 5 June 1578, just when his cardinal brother was tabling negotiations for His Highness' new royal wedding. The marriage was made public on 20 June 1579 and was solemnly repeated on 12 October. In the meanwhile she had been proclaimed "Most beloved daughter of the Venetian Republic", so, before a selective array of Venetian and Florentine nobility, Bianca Cappello was ceremoniously accompanied by the Venetian ambassadors to the foot of the grand ducal throne in the Salone in Palazzo Vecchio. Here she and the Duke were joined in matrimony by the Patriarch of Aquileia himself, Prince Grimani.

The Cardinal was not present; in his heart, he was never to accept the *fait accompli*. Neither was Lucrezia Grimani, Bianca's step mother, present; quite clearly she was not ready to witness her step-daughter's triumph.

As in a nice fairy story, we should like to end now, "and they lived happily ever after", but the story had neither a happy beginning nor a happy ending. In fact the memory of it is rather squalid.

Francesco I is remembered as the lover of the Venetian courtesan he then married. That is all. Especially in popular versions of satirical poems and *stornelli*, the event was stigmatised with unrepeatable crudeness of expression.

There remains little cognisance (or what does is undervalued) of his work as a scholar, as the creator of new institutions such as the Opificio delle Pietre Dure and particularly the Accademia della Crusca, as upgrader of the University of Pisa, the laicism of which he always defended, and as a keen collector and orderer of art treasures. (I do not, obviously, refer to more illuminated studies such as those I have already mentioned.) Just consider the artists who worked for him and who fashioned the sixteenth-century façade of Florence with works which are our joy and pride. The other side to his personality has hardly been considered: his scientific interests which at times sparked off bold enterprises, such as the search for copper in the Montecatini mines, or else practical undertakings like the courageous reclaiming of land, the compulsory cultivation of mulberries and sugar cane, the adoption of tuna fishing nets at Portoferraio and, especially, the uprating of the sea port of Livorno which Ammannati was entrusted with.

The years following the coroneting of the grand duchess were difficult ones, often distressing. Francesco had become thrifty, almost miserly, increasingly moody and irascible. He liked to isolate himself from his court and would spend lengthy periods at Pratolino in what appears to have been his favourite villa. Intrigue proliferated, due also to the presence on the scene of one of Bianca's brothers, a real scandalmonger. The meddling of the Jesuits in the climate advocating counter reform was getting more and more oppressive, even though the grand duke sometimes mustered enough energy to resist them. Above all, what tormented the new grand duchess was her great humiliation at not being able to provide her husband and the principate with an heir, especially after young Filippo's death. Hope dimmed after ridiculous expectations, farcical declarations and a continual, humiliating repetition of subdued denials. I am not sure how much of this was due to simulation and how much to hysteria.

I shall not give a summary of the years (nine in all) which ran between Bianca's marriage and her death, but, because the topic requires so, I will say that Bianca Cappello kept up an irreprehensible conduct over those years and it is not difficult to surmise that, had the opportunity presented itself, any charge against her would certainly not have remained secret. She always showed great benevolence to her husband's children and sought to make peace with the cardinal and with the court. She forced the quarrelsome Francesco, for instance, to allow poor Camilla Martelli to be present at the wedding of her daughter, Virginia. "She welcomed her at Palazzo Pitti", it was written, "and she honoured her." She was generous and charitable in an intelligent way. Her friendship with the passionate Florentine Saint Catherine confirms this, and she often turned to her for help for the sick and for a dowry for young girls. Such must have been her repute if Pope Sixtus V conferred the Golden Rose on her, which is the utmost pontifical honour granted to reigning princesses. Francesco and Bianca's deaths, which came about within one day of each other on 19 and 20 October 1587, would have had all the ingredients of a Machiavellian intrigue ending up in a double ferocious crime. That is, if medical investigations, recently confirmed by Pieraccini, as well, had not clearly demonstrated how the grand duke died of an attack of pernicious malaria and how his wife followed in his footsteps a day later with the same symptomatology. Together with them in their beautiful villa at Poggio a Caiano, which Sangallo had transformed from fortress into pleasant residence for Lorenzo, was Cardinal Ferdinando. With the excuse of a deer hunt, the grand duchess had made the umpteenth attempt at reconciliating the two brothers. Contemporaries went on about the hypothesis of the failure of Bianca's attempted poisoning of her brother-in-law due to his perspicacity and then of his bringing about the poisoning of the grand duke and of himself out of atonement, or perhaps it was the Cardinal's attitude that instigated such rumours? The pope himself said that "In the light of the Cardinal's presence, the world will comment greatly on this".

What is certain is the lack of Christian charity in a man who, though he had never taken the vows, was still a prince of the Holy Roman Church. No sooner had the grand duke closed his eyes, with Bianca in the throes of death just a few metres away, that the Cardinal, apart from making all the necessary arrangements to guarantee his immediate succession (which was logical and to be welcomed joyously by the whole population), ordered the destruction of anything reminiscent of Bianca, wishing in this way to wipe out all memory of her, just as he wiped out her name and arms wherever they were incised, thus wrecking precious works at the same time. When Grand Duke Francesco's State funeral was celebrated on 15 December, he lay alone on the high catafalque. By order of the Cardinal, Bianca's body had been immediately taken from Poggio a Caiano and inhumed outside the church in a tomb which has never been identified. So, the last Medicean prince of the *cinquecento* and Tuscany's first grand duke was buried (this title, so greatly coveted, had officially been conferred on him by Emperor Maximilian with Spain's consent). But, in his very solemn funeral ceremony, organised by the talented Buontalenti, his favourite architect, lay the seed of the last fruit of Florentine Mannerism, the ultimate gift that Florence made to culture and art … the art form that is opera, which, a few years later, had its fulfilment in acquiring a musical definition.

PINA MARZI CIOTTI

---

[1] Oh Ammannato, Oh Ammannato, / What a lot of marble you have ruined…"

CATHERINE AND MARIE DE' MEDICI
QUEENS OF FRANCE

Even in a rapid review, it would be an achievement to outline the figure of only one of the two French queens who were born into the House of the Medici, but to deal with both of them in a way which is not wholly incomplete is an almost desperate undertaking, for they both lived in historical periods which were extremely complicated and troubled. I shall, therefore, restrict myself to highlighting the main features of their characters, though I should particularly have liked to discuss these two personages at length. Indeed, the French sixteenth century reminds me of my first studies in this field that I undertook when, freshly graduated, I was able to spend a year at university in Paris, attending the lectures of some of the main French Renaissance scholars, such as Henri Chamard and Abel Lefranc, whilst that great historian of French literature, Gustave Lanson, was still in his full strength.

Among the many letters in our possession written by Catherine de' Medici, let us linger a while on one which dates from 1563. It is addressed to her son, Charles IX, referring to how he was to arrange his daily routine. This began with him getting up early at a set time, so that his subjects would know how to organise themselves and they would be aware of his intention to "remettre toutes choses selon Dieu et la raison". Given the progressive concentration of power in the hands of the sovereign, it is easily appreciated how the royal day was of particular importance and followed a solemn, complicated ritual, right since the time of Francis I, despite his frivolous, restless spirit, his mania for constantly new adventures, the many wars and the civilian and religious struggles. Let us imagine for an instant that we are in one of the royal residences, in the castle at Blois, for example, which particularly appeals to us on account of the evident traces of Italian art (in fact, the architect Domenico da Cortona lived at Blois from 1512 to 1530). Charles IX would get up before daybreak in both winter and summer. He would receive his shirt from the servant who had this honour and would start to get dressed, talking the while with the few intimate friends and collaborators who had access to his bedroom. Other important people would be assembling in an adjoining chamber. Once the king was dressed, a small altar would be set up in his room where he would pray and those waiting in the nearby room could join in. Then he would address each one in turn. After that, the sovereign would go into the room where the council was convening and where access was only granted to important people. The king would sit at the head of the table and the dauphin would stand beside him, with arrayed all around him the constable, admiral and a few secretaries. Here were decided prime affairs of state: wars, provisioning, problems with armaments and so on.

Catherine's letter to her son is a precious document in that it reveals her two main concerns: her children and the family - the continuity and dignity of the latter and the safeguarding of the dynasty in which, she acknowledged, lay the greatness of what had become her second homeland. The existence of this Florentine who had ended up on the throne of France was, from the start, plagued by tragic events. The daughter of Lorenzo de' Medici, Duke of Urbino and a cousin of Pope Clement VII, she became an orphan when just a few months old and was entrusted to the care of her maternal grandmother, from the Orsini family. She was brought up between both Florence and Rome. Then, she was put in a convent in Florence, where, what with her restiveness - and in the days of the siege, furthermore - she sparked off a revolution among her companions to the point that someone proposed taking drastic steps with regard to her behaviour. So it was that, at just fourteen, a political marriage was arranged for her. Her hand was given to Henry d'Orléans, second son of Francis I and, accordingly, nephew of Margaret of Angoulême, the true 'queen' of the French Renaissance.

At such a young age, Catherine found herself at the court of Francis I, who loved to surround himself with artists and literati, especially those of Italian origin. Among these, the Medici girl soon developed a liking for the Florentine Luigi Alamanni, the author of the poem, *La coltivazione*, dedicated to Francis I. He became a kind of right-hand man for her. But very soon she was exceedingly struck with admiration for the king's sister Margaret, as well. It was perhaps because of her, a tolerant spirit *par excellence*, that she came to appreciate the need for an agreement between Catholics and Protestants. A court such as the one she was part of widened her knowledge of Italian writers, starting with Boccaccio, at that time only recently translated into French by one of Margaret's secretaries, Antoine Le Maçon. With regard to this author and the Dauphine's admiration for his art, it says in the prologue to the *Heptaméron*: "je crois qu'il n'y a nulle de vous qui n'ait lu les *Cent Nouvelles* de Jean Boccace, nouvellement traduites d'italien en françois, desquelles le roi très-chrétien François premier de ce nom, Monseigneur le Dauphin, *Madame le Dauphine*, Madame Marguerite ont fait tant de cas, que si Boccace, du lieu où il était les eut pu ouir, il eut du ressusciter à la louange de telles personnes".

Catherine's husband, Henry, was very different from his father: shy, cantankerous, disgruntled. However it would appear that the young woman

57

was fond of her husband, though he did not feel the same way about her. The situation was very difficult: Henry, who had been on the throne since 1536, was completely in the sway of his mistress, Diane de Poitiers. Descending from a noble family, at the age of thirty she found herself a widow after the death of her husband, the Seneschal of Normandy and was several years Henry's senior. Diane had a cold, sculptural beauty which was perpetuated in the bronze statue *Diana the Hunter*, attributed to Goujon and also to Cellini. Intelligent and particularly shrewd, she was linked to the House of Guise and dominated the court, showing skill at intriguing, distributing prestigious posts and organising parties and tournaments. Catherine was soon defined by Diane as a "fille de marchand" and not even in the official painting by François Clouet does she appear beautiful, despite her big eyes. For ten years she bore no children and ran the risk of being repudiated. Paradoxically, in this situation it was Diane who made Henry more respectful towards his legitimate consort. Luckily, Catherine eventually became a mother and brought as many as ten children into the world. Relations were diplomatically impeccable between the two women who contended with each other for the king, but, in actual fact, the queen was in an awkward position. Diane, who had become duchesse de Valentinois, bedecked with jewels of the Crown, knew how to look after her beauty, even with the aid of physical exercise. She would get up early every morning and ride for many hours, then would return to bed to rest and read until midday, when her official commitments began. From the king she had received one of the loveliest châteaux in France, that of Chenonceaux on the river Cher. In the past century, it induced Flaubert to daydream in *Par les champs et par les grèves* when he wrote: "il y a encore à Chenonceaux, dans le chambre de Diane de Poitiers, le grand lit à baldaquin de la royale concubine, tout en damas blanc et cerise", referring also to the successive, legitimate proprietrix, Catherine: "je n'oserai pas seulement, de peur de les casser, toucher aux porcelaines de Catherine de Médicis qui sont dans la salle à manger, ni mettre mon pied dans l'étrier de François Ier...".

Heartened by her maternity, after a little time Catherine began to make her presence felt, as well. While Diane was celebrated by poets such as Du Bellay and Ronsard, Catherine became, first of all, the centre of attraction of the Italians who were already favoured by Francis I and his sister Margaret. During her reign, and successively for the favour that Marie continued to show Italians, more and more Italian expressions entered the French language, mostly referring to military and court-life, and were destined to remain. An example which is still typical is the word "courtisan", which derives from Baldassare Castiglione's *Il cortegiano ("The Courtyer")*, an opera which in France was very successful and had enormous influence, for

In this detail from a Brussels tapestry representing a tournament, Catherine de' Medici is portrayed together with her daughter Marguerite and her son-in-law Henri de Bourbon-Navarre, who subsequently became Henry IV of France and who married Marie de' Medici after repudiating Marguerite (Florence, Uffizi Gallery).

a long time considered the code of the perfect courtier.

Catherine brought to France an Italian commedia dell'arte troupe which was directed by Flaminio Scala and which was to meet with great success on the other side of the Alps. In 1548, Bibbiena's *Calandra* was staged at Lyons both for her and Henry II with great success. She was the one to transfer Francis I's library from Fontainebleau to Paris, and again it was Ronsard who alluded to these good services of hers when he had cause to remember the great cultural traditions of the Medici family:

> *Cette Reine d'honneur de telle race issue...*
> *Pour ne dégénérer de ses prémiers aieux,*
> *Soigneuse a fait chercher les livres les plus vieux*
> *Hébreux, Grecs et Latins, traduits et à traduire,*
> *Et par noble dépense elle en a fait reluire*
> *Le haut palais du Louvre afin que sans danger*
> *Le Français fût vainqueur du savoir étranger.*

As we know, the queen collected a group of maids-of-honour under her wing - the famous "flying squad" - which struck people for their beauty, not less for their intelligence and vivacity, as well as for the propriety of their conduct. It was Brantome himself, not easily satisfiable, to emphasise this. Among them was the famous Hélène de Surgères, whom Catherine proposed to Ronsard as a subject and for whom the great poet composed some of his loveliest poetry in the last period of his activity. From it all, I only need to remember the famous sonnet:

> *Quand vous serez bien vieille, au soir, à la chandelle,*
> *Assise auprès du feu, dévidant et filant,*
> *Direz, chantant mes vers, en vous émerveillant:*
> *"Ronsard me célébrait du temps que í'étais belle...".*

Catherine had given to Ronsard the priorship of Saint-Cosme-les-Tours, where the poet concluded his existence. In 1562, Ronsard wrote about her when she went to visit him with her sons Charles IX and Henry d'Anjou:

> *...Las! Ma Dame, en ce temps que le cruel orage*
> *Menace les Français d'un si piteux naufrage*
> *Que la grêle et la pluie et la fureur des cieux*
> *Ont irrité la mer de vents séditieux,*
> *Et que l'astre Jumeau ne daigne plus reluire,*
> *Prenez le gouvernail de ce pauvre navire,*
> *Et malgré la tempête, et le cruel effort*
> *De la mer et des vents conduissez-le à bon port...*

And when, later on, the same Ronsard composed the lyric, the *Bergerie dédiée à sa Majesté la Reine d'Ecosse*, he even went so far as to proclaim solemnly:

Si nous voyons le siècle d'or refait,
C'est du bienfait
De la Bergère Catherine.

And elsewhere, more explicitly:

Vous qui avez, forcant la destinée,
Si bien conduit cette trouble saison,
Vous qui avez par prudence et raison
Si dextrement la France gouvernée...

When Henry II was on the point of death in 1559, Catherine finally took her revenge on the rival who had caused her such suffering all those years, humiliating her at times, despite the formal respect and esteem that the sovereign showed her. However, even in these circumstances, she gave proof of that equilibrium and that sense of measure which were part of her temperament. Diane was immediately sent away and forced to return the Crown jewels, to give up Chenonceaux (where Catherine then carried out considerable work) and to retire to the château of Anet which was her property. Catherine's other son, Francis II, ascended the throne. He was dominated by his wife, Mary Stuart, so it was that his mother began to display all her energy, revealing her capacities of domination and intrigue. She found herself having to take on great responsibility in government in the middle of the violent contrast between the Guise and Montmorency families who contended influence at court in the period of the great religious struggles which lacerated France, putting her very existence at risk. It was the period when the "fille ainée de l'Eglise" oscillated between Catholicism and Reformation and this was while political difficulties of every kind - difficult relations with the Church and with other big nations - were creating a dangerous situation for the monarchy. It must be said that Catherine may not have been entirely aware of the perilous situation that the religious problem could have represented for the future of France. With her usual skill, she tried to manoeuvre between the opposing factions, until the famous massacre on the eve of the feast day of St Bartholomew came.

Of course, this threw an unsavoury light over her figure, as it is one of the grimmest instances of intolerance in history. It must, however, be said that Catherine did not act out of religious fanaticism, but in order to defend her country from political danger, even though she then tried to convince the

Church that she had actually acted in defence of Catholicism.

A tender, loving mother, who was also extremely ambitious for her sons' future, she intrigued at length to have Henry d'Anjou put on the Polish throne. She succeeded in doing so, but after a year her son returned to France consequent to his brother's death. Henry was, however, in conflict with the duc d'Alençon, so Catherine often had to travel across France to try and conciliate the two brothers. She tried to maintain that same equilibrium and agreement within the bosom of her family, too. But the queen died in 1589, having buried eight of her children.

Still out of her desire for grandeur and power, she had, far-sightedly (it must be admitted), given away her daughter Marguerite in 1572 to become the wife of Henri de Bourbon-Navarre, the future Henry IV. But, because of Marguerite's wanton behaviour and also because she failed to give Henry any children, the marriage was dissolved, permitting the sovereign to marry Marie de' Medici.

Used by Catherine for political ends were also her relations with the literati under her protection. We have mentioned the "bergerie" that she got Ronsard to compose; well, the celebrations that took place at Fontainebleau on that occasion had, in her intentions, the purpose of bringing together those who had clashed in the recent violent struggles on religious grounds, in order to foster the formation of a different, more serene climate. Likewise, at other times, she made use of the same poet to try and ingratiate Queen Elizabeth of England. Neither did others among the foremost French writers elude these manoeuvres which the Queen exercised on the cultural life of her times (even though her ends were often political). Etienne Jodelle, for example (according to the Italian critic, Enea Balmas, who is the greatest scholar on him, Etienne saw in her "the source of all authority and power ... the dispenser of any favour or privilege") even goes so far as to sing her praises;

> *Quand je te vois sur toi porter toute la France*
> *Comme Atlas fait le ciel, ton chef Royal baissant*
> *Sous un fardeau qui va le faix du ciel passant:*
> *Car l'un d'ordre et d'accord justement se balance,*
> *L'autre est plein de discord, désordre et insolence,*
> *Abus, erreur, fureur, que tu vas régissant,*
> *Pourtant dessous ton fils les hauts coeurs régissant,*
> *Et rabaissant les vils par conseils et prudence...*

It is true that these expressions, and numerous others that we could quote, are to a large extent the fruit of an adulation which is not disinterested, but apart from the fact that in certain instances their sincerity is documented,

Henry II of France in a portrait by François Clouet (Florence, Pitti Gallery).

it is, however, always true that the queen knew how to exploit the more authoritative representatives of culture at that time to back up her work. In any case, this points to her skill in governing, her trying to turn all the forces available to advantage in her political actions. After all, in a century of violent politico-religious struggle, Catherine de' Medici showed great strength of spirit in overcoming extremely difficult family conditions. First and foremost, she lived for her children, who often were the cause of bitter disappointment, and she occupied her position as Queen with great dignity and propriety, even though her very condition as a foreigner placed her in a particularly delicate position right from the start. Of course, she was an ambitious woman, but for her family, above all. She was an intriguer, too, but in a historical period when intrigue was at the very base of political life, as state power was concentrated more and more exclusively into the hands of the sovereign; that same private council that was referred to at the beginning of this article is to do with family, but, when all is said and done, decisional power is always in the hands of the king. As far as Catherine was concerned, the fact that her main ambitions coincided with her defence of the family's greatness and that of the state cannot be dismissed. In truth, at certain times, such as after the death of Henry II, the destiny of the state was completely in her hands. On her death, the poet Bertaut gave a good interpretation of the feelings of gratitude for her pacifying labours when he wrote, "avec elle - est morte, du mesme lit, la paix universelle". As we said before, Catherine had tried to make links with Henri de Bourbon-Navarre by marrying her daughter off to him, but once he had become king under the name of Henry IV (the Bourbon dynasty began with him), he ended up by repudiating his wife. But, the king was obviously destined to marry into the Medici family in any case, because, wishing to obtain legitimate heirs, he married Marie de' Medici, the daughter of Francis I, Grand Duke of Tuscany, and of Joanna of Austria.

Rubens' imposing representations at the Louvre portray various moments in Marie's life, beginning when she was twenty-five with her nuptials to a mature though vigorous Henry, desirous of an heir. And Marie, whom we see portrayed in all her grandeur by the Flemish painter, did give him one, but the joys of motherhood were briefly lived for the Medicean bride, as she soon found out that, within a month of this birth, the dauphin had acquired an illegitimate brother, born to one of Henry's numerous lovers, Henriette d'Entragues. Indeed, if Marie brought six children into the world, Henry had eight illegitimate ones by his many lovers. In order to remember the various mothers, the king even had to resort to a biographical list!

Henry's dissolute life was certainly the cause of great bitterness for Marie in the ten years that she lived with her husband before he fell under

Henry IV of France in a portrait by Pourbus (Florence, Pitti Palace, former Royal Apartments).

Ravaillac's dagger. Apart from his sensuality, the merits of this sovereign are not few, as, with his adept policy of tolerance and with his political equilibrium, he was able to steer the country towards a great future. At the bottom of his soul, he had a generous spirit which induced him to concern himself with his subjects' happiness (even in the private sphere). He yearned for a life devoid of material suffering after such long years of war and grieving. By defining him as *Le Vert galant,* vox populi displayed a true sympathy with his figure. His memory remains bound to the Edict of Nantes, which was a great act of shrewdness, apart from humanity. In it, whilst he was trying to meet the wishes of the Huguenots, his old companions of his youth and of so many struggles and wars, he established that France was a Catholic nation, however evident the political motives of his conversion were after his long militation in the ranks of the reformers with whom he had fought and suffered.

With her husband's death (though he felt no love for her, he esteemed her for her qualities), Marie found herself having to put to the test her energy and equilibrium, her discernment and her skill at protecting the interests of the Dauphin, the future Louis XIII. A prudent woman, she was immediately anxious to come to an agreement with Spain, signing a peace treaty. Being less gifted than Catherine, when she found that she had to battle with the princes of the kingdom, with Condé first and foremost, she inevitably leant on the people in her confidence, starting with a Florentine, Concino Concini, who had been a follower of hers ever since her marriage and who had married the daughter of the Queen's wet nurse, Leonora Galigai, into the bargain. Concini was a man of great ambition and uncommon energy. Though at first he had managed to assert his authority at court, he then gradually became hateful to the sovereign herself, owing to his craving for grandeur and to the fact that he sided against the aristocracy - he a foreigner - and he ended up being murdered, whilst his wife fell a victim to popular loathing.

After all, it is understandable that Marie confided in a man (and an extremely sagacious one into the bargain). But Concini had succeeded in reaching such an elevated social position that he aroused strong resentment. It must not be overlooked that Richelieu himself had his first experiences with him (he had known him for a long time and he reminded him of his distant fatherland). Contributing to make Concini an unlikeable figure was also, perhaps, the fact that he surrounded himself with Italian staff, thus emphasising that the Queen's trust was placed principally in foreigners; not a difficult subject of dispute in the hands of adversaries.

Certain it is that, with Concini's death, Marie's power began to degenerate, even though, when her son, Louis XIII, ascended the throne, he

Cardinal Richelieu in a portrait by Champaigne (Paris, Louvre).

pronounced his desire that his mother should continue to be involved with the government of the kingdom.

The judgement that history has passed on Marie's policies during her regency is rather controversial. The book of an Italian scholar, Salvo Mastellone, has made a significant contribution of clarification. Entitled *La reggenza di Maria de' Medici*, it is published in Florence. By means of a thorough examination of documents, he demonstrates that Marie de' Medici and her minister boosted the assertion of royal power. From this stems the resistance encountered and also the obstacles of various nature that the foreign queen had to overcome in order to reach her goal, at times making the most of the help supplied by ministers of Henry IV's time. One cannot fail to admit that, if the consequences of the long struggles between the aristocracy and the Third State, between the clergy and the representatives of the sovereign power were that the latter emerged reinforced, and if they contributed in giving shape to the same in an ever more decisive way, then credit is also due to Marie and her minister, due to her activity and her commitment in what she held to be her duty as a mother and as the sovereign.

After the death of Concini, Richelieu's rise in status seemed at first to betoken the triumph of a protégé of hers and consequently yet another affirmation of her power. But very soon things took another turn. The cardinal's personality was too vigorous and he was not averse to carrying arms, respectful of his military past. Despite Marie's efforts to defend her power, various incidents followed one another over a considerable period of time, leading the way to her progressive decline. First she would retire to Blois or Angoulême, then she would resume her place in political life, until her differences with Richelieu took shape very forcefully. When Louis XIII was ill at a certain time and his mother tended him lovingly, it would seem that she wrested a promise from him that he would keep the cardinal at a distance. Such a concession is easily explainable in a son up against filial affection, but here the government of a state is involved and not private affairs. Besides, Richelieu's personality was rather too powerful, whilst the sovereign could not forgo the great minister's industry. In the struggle between the two, the Queen came out the loser. She believed she could muster up various subjects discontented with the cardinal's operations and of whom there was no lack, but they only managed to disrupt what, in a certain sense, could be considered the Queen's party. Marie did not accept defeat. With her unyielding character, she counted on being able to continue intriguing from abroad, but, in 1642, death caught up with her in Cologne.

A sad twilight it was, partly due to her quarrelsome character. After all, Richelieu was, to a certain extent, a creature of her own making and the cardinal had great trouble in mollifying her, at times without success and often clashing with her. Of course, we cannot talk about her in the same terms as the poet Bertaut had done regarding Catherine, which we mentioned earlier on. It must be borne in mind that Marie had been left motherless while still a child, with Bianca Cappello for step-mother, who had other thoughts on her mind rather than concerning herself with Joanna of Austria's orphan. And though we cannot say about her what a contemporary stated about Catherine - "the Dauphine studies diligently and is very well-read, especially in Greek, which amazes everyone" - at least she was culturally aware because of the environment Marie was born into, especially with regard to Italian culture. She could be compared to Catherine neither from this point of view as the latter, according to Henri Estienne, "took *une petite Italie* with her to the court of France". But, think of the relationship Marie had with Malherbe, for example, who had written his first grand ode for her arrival in Paris in 1600, after her marriage had been celebrated by proxy in Florence:

Aujourd'hui nous est amenée
Cette princesse que la foi
D'amour ensemble et d'Hyménée
Destine au lit de nostre roi.
La voici, la belle Marie,
Belle merveille d'Etrurie,
Qui fait confesser au soleil,
Quoi che l'âge passé raconte,
Que du ciel, depuis qu'il y monte,
Ne vint jamais rien de pareil...

After Henry IV's death, Malherbe was amply protected by the queen and enjoyed a certain atmosphere of sympathy. He owed this protection to his relationship with the Guise and Condé families, as well. Honoured by Marie's trust, Malherbe paid her back with true loyalty. From among the Italians, the queen insisted on having Giambattista Marino in Paris and he met with great success among French scholars, even finding admirers and imitators among poets such as Saint-Amant. Thanks to Marie's benevolence, Marino was completely at ease in Paris, so much so that he wrote to Lorenzo Scoto in 1615, "I am living like a lord here and I have so much money that I do not know what to do with it. The *reine* has departed, leaving it up to me to follow her or stay. I do not know what I shall do but I am tempted to stay here and pass these three months studying and perfecting *Adone* with a nuptial song concerning this wedding". He was referring to the nuptial song *La Francia consolata* for Louis XIII's wedding to Anne of Austria, which took place that same year (1615). Marino also adulated Leonora Concini, a confidant of the queen, as he was convinced (and he told her so in a letter) that "it is difficult to enter the innermost grace of H.M. without the aid of an introduction from you".

So, when in 1622 *Adone* was published in Paris, Marino felt obliged to dedicate it to Louis XIII and at the same time to Marie: "That a mother should take part in the glory and praise imparted to her son is a truly divine and human law. That she should share in the praise and glory contained in this volume, in particular, is a just thing out of respect to her and also to me. Out of respect to her, as Her Majesty is the earth which has produced such a fine plant and also the plant that has given birth to so noble a fruit, all honour must be attributed no less to her, who is the cause, than to him who is the effect.

As far as I am concerned, I owe everything to her and my present situation rests on her completely as, on account of her official kindness, I find myself in the present service of this court. As I recognise the growth of my fortunes due to her protection, so do I feel obliged to acknowledge the courtesies received...as well as the fact that the work that I dedicate to her is almost a register of her grand deeds".

It is often written that Catherine and Marie both tended towards political intrigue and we are certainly not going to deny it, but it must be borne in mind how, especially in Marie's times, such intrigue thrived in life at court to the same degree that the conception of the state which was to prevail fully at the time of the Sun King grew. Above all, at the points in time when they held the reins of the state, both queens had to defend themselves first of all from a thousand intrigues which were spun around them, from adversaries and courtiers in search of favours and from the calumny which was put around for personal benefit (consider the great amount of libel against Marie). They also had to fight against the Church on one hand and other states such as Austria, Spain and England on the other, whilst the aristocracy reacted to any act which resolved in the limitation or reduction of their privileges.

So it is that these two Florentine princesses appear to us in a more human light, despite all the political errors that they might have made. Especially if, liberating the images of traditional regal splendour, we linger a while to consider certain aspects of their womanhood which were so often sorely tried, and in particular the anxiety for their children's fortunes and the constancy displayed in defending the continuity of the high office that Fate had entrusted them with.

CARLO PELLEGRINI

VITTORIA DELLA ROVERE

On 25 October 1623, a princely procession set off from the Pitti Palace for a solemn baptism. Countess Costanza della Gherardesca, the wife of Giovan Francesco Mamiani, carried in her arms a richly-dressed baby girl, bedecked with precious jewels. Pages and gentlemen accompanied her along the Vasari Passage to reach Palazzo Vecchio, where a hundred and thirty ladies had gathered in their sumptuous satin and velvet gowns, full of puffs and frills. A long file of forty-two coaches, each pulled by six or eight horses, carried the illustrious personages from Palazzo Vecchio to the Cathedral and the Baptistery of San Giovanni, where the christening was conducted in pomp. Standing in for the pope as godfather was Cardinal Borromeo, and everything was handled with ceremony and magnificence and with the fastidiousness that the etiquette of that century required.

The baby to whom so much honour was paid was Maria Vittoria Della Rovere. She was fifteenth months old and had already been duly christened at her birth, which had come about on 7 February 1622 in Pesaro. Her new christening, imparted to her so solemnly in San Giovanni in Florence, was not, as some may think, in homage to the city's patron saint, but an affirmation of her "Florentineness" and, above all, the sealing of a pact between the Medici and Della Rovere families because little Vittoria was already considered the bride of the future Grand Duke Ferdinando, who, at that time, was all of thirteen and a blood-cousin of the baby girl.

Her life certainly did not get off to a happy start, for right from her birth, family circumstances sacrificed her to reasons of state. She was the daughter of Claudia de' Medici and Federico Ubaldo Della Rovere, the degenerate son of that excellent prince who had been Francesco Maria, born to him in 1604 by Livia di Ippolito Della Rovere. Since an early age, Federico Ubaldo showed himself up for what Grottanelli defined as a delinquent and Pieraccini as a degenerate. He rebelled against any kind of discipline and was insensitive to any moral constraint. Given over to all kinds of vice, he took pleasure in the company of rogues and would pass his nights in revelry or in provoking passers-by in the streets, giving a most distressing show of degradation and corruption. After various attempts at putting his life back on decorous rails more in keeping with his name and family, there were hopes that an early marriage might induce him to change his lifestyle. As a child, he had already been engaged to Claudia of Ferdinando I de' Medici in 1609. In 1621, it was decided to celebrate the marriage to give the young rake the backing of an authoritative family. The wedding took place in Florence on 29 April in Villa Baroncelli, but there was neither pomp nor joy because of Grand Duke Cosimo II's recent death (at barely the age of thirty, but he had insisted that his sister's wedding should take place all the same because it was a political commitment) and because knowledge about the young bridegroom's previous capers did not encourage too many illusions as to the likely success of the marriage. Indeed, after the first days of joyous festivity of the bridal couple, Federico resorted to his disorderly life, inducing the complaints of Claudia, who showed her dissatisfaction and disapproval to her husband, whereupon he took umbrage (once he even slapped her), and she complained to his family who, however, were not able to make much impression on him. And things got worse when Francesco Maria retired from government, leaving the responsibility to his son, who then seized on his increased authority to rid himself of the wise but importunate counsellors whom his father had placed at his side. He replaced them with people of quite another sort, suited to him, who was always giving himself up to his lowest instincts.

At a certain point he joined a company of actors, among whom there was a certain Argentina whom he fell madly in love with. So much so, in fact, that he stooped to playing humble parts in the company in order to be near to her, ready to recite vulgar gags. He finally led the woman to live in a wing of the ducal palace which he often visited, either on his own or with friends, for parties or scandalous orgies. It was indeed following one of these that, on the morning of 29 June 1623, while a hunting party were waiting for him, he was found dead in his bed, with the door locked from the inside. He was just over eighteen years old. There was talk of apoplexy, of poison which perhaps had been sent by the Medici to loosen that shameful connection, even of the malignant influence of the stars. One thing was certain; his death was the mark of little Vittoria's new destiny. At that time, she was little more than a year of age.

As soon as news of Federico's death reached Florence, Count Orso di Elci and the Knight Commander Andrea Cioli, Grand Chancellor, omnipotent personage at the Medici court, both hastened to Urbino, officially to express their condolences to the bereaved father, but in point of fact to regularise Claudia's position and take the opportunity offered by the circumstances of benefiting the Tuscan Grand Duchy. The Medici had laid their eyes on the duchy of Urbino some time ago and especially on its wealth and collections. It would be an adroit move if a tie could be created between the two houses. It was obvious that Claudia should return to Florence, and in fact she asked for nothing more. So it was that, after Francesco Maria (in the vain hope of a male heir) had satisfied himself that she was not pregnant, she left on

72

An exuberant picture of Vittoria della Rovere in the years of her youth (Sustermans, Florence, Corsini Gallery).

14 August 1623, accompanied by don Lorenzo de' Medici and a vast retinue. And as her grief for the death of her husband was distinctly not very great (one could hardly expect it to be) and did not blur her sight of concrete assets, she took the jewels away with her, even those belonging to the Della Rovere coronet which she had been allowed to use, saying that her husband had

donated them to her in a moment of tenderness. She refused to return them, however much Francesco Maria (and also the Medici) tried to convince her to do so. The business dragged on until 1631 with letters, envoys and negotiations; little is known about the outcome. Claudia's journey took her through the Casentino district, with stops at Verna and Camaldoli, right on to Florence, where her grand duke nephew and her grand duchess mother welcomed her to Palazzo Pitti. Journals of the time do not mention whether this homecoming was particularly moving. Probably it was not, both because the protocol and strict rules of etiquette cooled any outburst of feeling and because Claudia had nothing to complain about at the moment and, anyway, she was rather self-seeking and arid of sentiment, as is demonstrated not only by the episode of the jewels, but also by her future attitude with regard to little Victoria. The latter had been kept innocent and unaware at Urbino, whilst Francesco Maria and the Florentine ambassadors held long, difficult negotiations to decide on her fate. Much tact, skill and adroitness were needed to clinch the deal. But, in the end, so as to remove the child from the clutches of the Roman court which yearned for dominion over the Urbino Duchy, the Florentines managed to persuade Francesco Maria, fraught with grief at his son's death and suffering from gout, to make out his will in favour of his grandchild. He assured her all the allodial estate of the duchy (which was not insignificant, consisting in mansions, furnishings, works of art, jewels, silverware and ready money) and promising her hand to Grand Duke Ferdinando II. The agreement was stipulated at Casteldurante on 20 September 1623. But how and where was Vittoria to live? Not even on this point would the Medici give way. She was to be educated in Florence and entrusted to the care of her grandmother, Madame Christine, Cosimo II's mother (who at that time held the regency of Florence together with her daughter-in-law, Maria Magdalena of Austria), rather than her paternal grandmother, Livia Della Rovere, who would have liked to be responsible. So it was that Vittoria left for Florence to follow her new, unhappy destiny. The journey took place with the usual formalities and the customary etiquette.

The two grand duchesses were waiting for her at the Villa Bandini al Paradiso and the young grand duke at the Gates of the Fabbrica Nuova, but Countess Costanza della Gherardesca, whose husband, Francesco Giovanni Mamiana had gone to great lengths for Vittoria's kinsfolk, solemnly delivered her to Madame Christine at Palazzo Pitti.

We have already talked about the christening, which followed a short time after Vittoria's arrival as if to mark the opening of a new life. The child was immediately placed in the convent of the Crocetta, to which Claudia had retired as was the custom for widows. Mother and daughter had a whole apartment at their disposal, two gardens and a substantial following of maids-of-honour and attendants. Vittoria also had two little cousins to play with, Maria Maddelena and Maria Cristiana. But right from the beginning, in the restricted life of the convent, full of pettiness, qualms and obduracy, Vittoria's disagreeable and pig-headed character began to take shape and was to remain with her her whole life long.

Her childhood was not happy, neither could it be. She missed a father's guidance, the warmth of a family and the tenderness of a mother. Claudia never showed any concern for the child, born to a husband of such bad habit and so unloved. This sentimental detachment increased even more when, in 1626, she contracted a new marriage with her mother's brother, Leopold, Archduke of the Tyrol and Archbishop of Passau and Strasbourg, who, attracted by her conspicuous dowry, renounced the purple and led her to Innsbruck as his wife. But the new marriage was not happy either. Leopold, vulgar and avid for wealth, had no passion other than hunting, to which he dedicated most of his time, neglecting his young bride who tried to make up for her sentimental solitude by devoting herself to affairs of state and welcoming Italian literati and artists to the court. Among these were Lorenzo Lippi, a painter, who dedicated to her the mock-heroic poem, *Il Malmantile riacquistato*, publishing it under the pseudonym of Perlone Zipoli. She also did her utmost to bring benefit to the children born to her new marriage.

But Claudia thought nothing or very little of the child left in Florence. Although she was a great letter-writer, in her copious correspondence we have no letter addressed to her daughter, whilst there are two of the child Vittoria's letters to her grandmother Livia della Rovere, where she laments her mother's scant love for her. There is another one, written on occasion of Francesco Maria's death (1631) in which she expresses the same complaint. And if (as is likely) at least the first was dictated or even merely suggested by some adult, that does not change the situation. It is certain that, after their separation, mother and child saw each other no more and, though Claudia made frequent, often lengthy journeys, she never felt the urge to return to Florence, not even for her daughter's wedding. Devoid of a mother's love, did Vittoria find human warmth and affection in the family she became part of?

The situation at court was rather delicate. After Ferdinando I's death, his widow, Christine of Lorraine, held the regency with a council of authoritative ministers during her son Cosimo II's minority. After the latter's premature death, Maria Magdelena of Austria joined her mother-in-law as regent of the state and guardian of Ferdinando II. History tells us a great deal about these two women to whose care Vittoria was entrusted, neither of whom were rich in either intelligence or good-heartedness.

Christine of Lorraine, granddaughter of King Henry II and Catherine de' Medici is a figure entirely dominated by religious fanaticism. Her life was spun out among pilgrimages, religious offices, processions, professions of vows and the founding of monasteries, while her religious sentiment was mixed with superstition and a blind faith in amulets, devils and witches. She is responsible for the allowances to converts, so you never saw such a mass of people (Turks, Arabs and Jews) who gaily passed to the Catholic religion for personal gain. The people she surrounded herself with (friars, priests, nuns, self-seekers and ambitious courtiers) had a negative influence on her and it was then that the decadence of the state began, due also to her administrative ignorance. Her daughter-in-law, Maria Magdalena of Austria, Cosimo II's widow, also contributed to this downfall. She was of an authoritarian, strong-willed disposition and so found herself in friction with her mother-in-law, being a greater intriguer and more interested in state affairs, even when the council demanded by Ferdinando I in his will was in operation. However, this was quickly dispensed with by both mother- and daughter-in-law and the government turned over to mediocre people dominated by that gentleman Andrea Cioli, who caused such great damage to the state. In their domestic lives, each of the grand duchesses wished to rise above the other and, as they were both foreigners, in foreign policy it was natural that they should side with their countries of origin (France and Austria) and that at times unpleasant disputes should arise, also in the presence of the ambassadors of other states who then related the happenings.

But what both of them agreed on (even too much so) were their bigotry, their love of pomp and their zeal for appearances and etiquette. The two women's vanity was patent not only in the luxury of their court, but also in the squandering that was effected on every occasion, whether in mascherades, theatrical comedies, balls or hunts. So much so, in fact, that the whole treasure that Ferdinando I had left was burnt up over the eight regency years, despite the clause that nothing should be touched except in cases of dire necessity. And there were even sneaking suspicions that many religious works were dictated more by the desire to show off than by a deep sense of Christian charity, of which the grand duchesses exhibited scarce endowment in many circumstances. Such as when they persecuted Livia Vernazza, whom Don Giovanni de' Medici had married even though of humble origin and dubious morality and who, after Giovanni's death (1621), was relegated to the Forte del Belvedere for sixteen years. They had her son taken away from her when just a child and succeeded in having the marriage declared null and void so as to cheat him out of his inheritance in favour of the House of Medici. In this setting, where words and exterior practices did not correspond

Claudia de' Medici, mother of Vittoria, who showed so little affection and concern for her daughter (Sustermans, Florence, Pitti Palace, former Royal Apartments).

Maria Magdalena of Austria, Vittoria's bigotted, authoritarian mother-in-law, in a youthful portrait (attributed to Sustermans, Florence, Corsini Gallery).

to deeds, where questions of precedence and privilege were of such importance, Vittoria grew up and spent her life. Even though the two grand duchesses loved her, they educated her their own way. Right from her infancy, they instilled in her ideas of grandeur. She was called "the bride", as if to remind her every day about her future destiny as grand duchess. Just like Geltrude, the Nun from Monza in Alessandro Manzoni's "The Betrothed", her whole life unwound in the prospect of the authority and future position that was to be hers one day. If we add to that her education, the examples shown her of intransigence and of a religiousness more apparent than it was real, then it is no wonder that Vittoria grew up so haughty and supercilious, full of ambition, vanity and superficiality and with such an exceedingly difficult character.

Her marriage to Ferdinando which, as we know, had been arranged on 20 September 1624 when little more than a baby was celebrated privately in Palazzo Pitti on 2 August 1634, basically at Christine's wish as she was by then getting on in years (Maria Magdalena was already dead). But just as Vittoria had been baptised twice, so she was married twice and her true marriage was celebrated and consumed on 6 April 1637.

Chronicles tell us that the festivities were not so grand. All the same, we have many descriptions and song lyrics, scenic productions, choreographies and musical entertainments, the most important of which was entitled *Le nozze degli Dei* in five acts by Giovanni Carlo Coppola. It was performed in the courtyard of the Pitti Palace with a great display of machinery and splendid costumes, setting in motion all the gods of heaven, sea and earth, nymphs, satyrs, Cyclops, harpies, winds and clouds to celebrate the glories of the Medici and Della Rovere houses and wish good luck on the very young bridal couple. Ferdinando was twenty-six, Vittoria fifteen. But the marriage was not happy. Too different were their characters and too intolerant was Vittoria, who, brought up in preparation for her future greatness, did nothing except exert her authority and flaunt her origins as princess of Urbino. She was very proud of her latter status, partly in consideration of the wealth that she had brought in her dowry and which had been transferred to Florence in 1631, after Francesco Maria's death, when the Della Rovere dynasty had been extinguished.

It is a known fact that since childhood, since the period of their engagement, there had been misunderstandings between her and Ferdinando which lasted their lifetimes, even though, officially, they tried to save appearances, turning out together in public. There was even an eighteen-year period when the couple had no intimate relations, whether owing to the grand duke's irritation at presumably having been disturbed in an intimate stance with a page, or to hers in punishment for his unfaithfulness, it is not known. In any case, as the historian Pieraccini observes, many are the episodes showing the aridity of Vittoria's senses and feelings. Even during Ferdinando's fatal illness, she only visited him once at his express request.

Ferdinando, on the other hand, oppressed as he had been in his childhood and adolescence by the two regent grand duchesses, had a mild, conciliating character. Chroniclers narrate that, at the coronation ceremony which took place in Palazzo Vecchio when he was a child of eleven, he sat under the canopy with his grandmother and mother on either side. There is a painting representing him in this pose. Well then, one could say that he lived his whole life in the shade of the grand duchesses - one on this side, one on the other - flanked by them and, unfortunately, infelicitously influenced; so much so that the best period of his reign was after their deaths. In actual fact, he was a man born more for study and the sciences than for government. Uncertain in politics and tending to steer a middle course between Spain, France and Austria, he did not obtain the advantages that he had hoped for from his neutrality. He tried to better his country in the spheres of agriculture and commerce which were flagging. Surrounding himself with men of high science such as Galileo (of whom he was a pupil), Evangelista Torricelli, Vincenzo Viviani and Francesco Redi, he specifically devoted himself to the physical and mathematical sciences. Following his natural inclinations, he invented or perfected scientific instruments and, together with his brother, Leopoldo, he founded the Accademia del Cimento. Neither did he forget the arts; he instituted the famous collection of great artists' self-portraits, enlarged Palazzo Pitti and had some of the rooms decorated by Pietro da Cortona and Giovanni da San Giovanni. In his final years he collected quite a few sculptures and paintings, even fostering music.

At his side, Vittoria showed no evidence of those qualities which would have made a real sovereign of her and, what is more, she had none of those interests her husband enjoyed and which could have drawn the couple together more forcefully.

If Vittoria was not happy as a wife (though the fault lies more with her than with Ferdinando), she had no luck in motherhood either. In 1639, she gave birth to a son who lived but a few hours and another baby girl died at birth in 1641. Finally in 1642 was born Cosimo, the future grand duke. It was only in 1660 (possibly the fruit of her reconciliation with Ferdinando) that the second son, Francesco Maria, arrived, later to become cardinal. But Cosimo gave his mother more worries than joys. Defined as very close, introverted, sad and moody, he was the true figure of the narrow-minded, bigoted prince, with but a few, restricted ideas. And as at that time marriage was evidently considered a remedy for all evils, if Federico Ubaldo of Urbino had been given a wife to calm his fiery spirit, Cosimo was given a wife to shake him up and overcome his inertia. The most ebullient, and profligate princess in Europe, Marguerite-Louise d'Orléans, granddaughter of Marie de' Medici and Henry IV was chosen for him. She marred him, but with her cousin Charles of Lorraine in her heart, and as she kept this love for the whole of her life, she put the court and her husband through the mill with scandals, sudden disappearances and illicit love affairs with people of all kinds. She continually stated her hatred for Tuscany, the Medici and Cosimo, until the latter had the idea of sending her back to France, where she continued her disorderly life without a thought for her three children, left behind in Florence.

One can well imagine what the relations between mother- and daughter-in-law were like. The one all bigotry and religious practices, hypocrisy and human respect; the other beautiful, young, vivacious, devoid of moral deterrents, who, out of spite, delighted herself in doing anything that came into her head, humiliating her husband and mother-in-law, who was doomed to defeat in the clash with her daughter-in-law because the people instinctively felt more sympathy towards the young woman who broke the bonds of etiquette without any sulkiness, rather than towards the old grand duchess who was so hard and inflexible, completely engrossed in her religious manias and her world of privileges and frivolous questions of priority.

In fact, Vittoria could hardly not suffer from the example and influence of the two regents under whose guidance she had been brought up. Like them, she had surrounded herself with unworthy people, priests and friars who lorded it over the court. But the religion that she practised with such fervour, instead of opening up her mind and her heart to noble notions of goodness and of deepening her sentiment or of inducing her to comprehension and indulgence, showed itself practically only in exterior forms, making her a slave to scruple, doggedness and superstitions, not detached from a deep sense of pride and vanity. Indeed, Pieraccini says that she was rather mundane by nature, prone to a heedless society life, and that her religion was only a useless adjunct, an effect of her background. Like the two regent grand duchesses, she was also said to promote religious works more out of exhibitionism than generosity and Christian charity. The greater her age, the more her bigotry and rigidity with regard to custom grew; in fact, she had her own secret service to find out exactly what was happening in the various families, even the most intimate and delicate deeds. She instigated her son Cosimo III (she was always a hapless counsellor to him) to inflict pitiless, severe punishment, with no indulgence for certain human weaknesses.

This rigidity and this unbending vision of life were curiously accompanied by a deep sense of pride in her origins and position and by vanity which was expressed in the most frivolous and superficial ways. She had a devotion to herself and her persona; suffice it to consider the great quantity of sculptures, paintings and medallions which she had herself portrayed in. Here she is vestal and Magdalene, both young and old, and there even the Madonna in the Holy Family, with little Cosimo in her arms as the figure of Jesus. Of these two contrasting aspects of Vittoria - religiousness and vanity - her rich epistolary is evidence. There are letters where she exerts her influence in recommending churchmen, or she negotiates the founding of religious institutes, or she keeps herself busy conferring parishes and canonries, or she requests some precious religious reliquary. There are others, just as numerous and beseeching, where she applies all over the place for information on new fashions, requesting fans of recent manufacture, discussing the setting of certain jewels, searching for the perfumes which were then all the rage and putting a commitment and preciseness into all which would have been worthy of a higher cause.

Contrasting her affirmations of Christian humility and self-denial, few princesses were lovers of pomp, luxury and entertainment like she was. Her court was very rich, her clothes and furnishings lavish and refined, her parties, balls and masquerades complete with all the sumptuousness that the seicento was capable of. She embellished Baroncelli's villa, bought by Maria Magdalena to the delight of the grand duchesses, who then called it Villa Imperiale, and enriched it with flowered gardens. She was not short of a certain taste for beautiful things and did not completely lack culture. She knew French and Spanish and, perhaps in her strive for glory, was patroness of a women's literary academy, "Le Assicurate", set up in Siena in 1654, which took her for its emblem. Of rather too modest intellect to be able to understand and appreciate the world of Galileo and the other scientists centred around Ferdinando II, she did not wish to appear impervious to the traditional patronage of the Medici and turned her interest and protection to people who did not deserve it at all. Benedetto Menzini and Gian Andrea Moniglia were two poets, the one more venomous than the other, who flung insults, abuse and terrible accusations at each other, only to join up in their hatred for another scholar of the time, Antonio Magliabechi.

Menzini was an author of satirical works where he railed at the corrupt customs of the times and at the many mediocre fortunates who achieved high ranking without merit. His satire, however, was not serene and objective, but dictated by the envy deriving from his presumption and from the fact that he considered he had been betrayed by men and by fate. His favourite target was Moniglia who, at that time, was having great success with his scenic productions. He was omnipotent at court, protected as he was by the grand duchess, and therefore he did not hesitate to pursue his personal enemies, even forcing them to flee Florence. Among his "victims" there was also Magliabechi; he may have been meritorious for his erudition, but, as a man, was truly despicable; a spy, a slanderer, a pervert.

Selvaggia Borghini, a poetess who had sung of Vittoria's wedding, earned her sympathy and support, too. But we are still in that mediocre world that the grand duchess neither wanted nor was able to shake herself free from. On account of her paucity of spirit and intellect, Vittoria was not a very significant figure in the history of the House of the Medici. She has been accused of having contributed to the family's decadence, and this happened more because of her negative qualities as a woman and princess than, as some would have it, for her erroneous tendencies as far as the government was concerned (Ferdinando always kept her well away from affairs of state), or for the scarce agreement there had always been between her and her husband, or because he considered her (rightly so) unfit for that task. At the most, she damaged the state with the limited, narrow-minded way in which she brought up Cosimo III. Because of his weak character, he allowed himself to be influenced by his mother whom he trusted blindly and from whom he had inherited his worst side, which, unfortunately, was revealed in his ill-fated government both before and after Vittoria's death. So it was that the state fell to its doom.

Vittoria died in 1694 at Pisa, where she had gone for a little respite in her poor conditions of health. On this occasion, too, Cosimo II showed deference towards his mother with the solemn funeral celebrated in San Lorenzo's Basilica in Florence, with the citizens given three days' notice so that "the eternal, glorious memory of Her Most Serene Highness the Duke's mother could be honoured with solemn, funereal pomp". The stately funeral took place, not only in the presence of the court but also of the whole population who had been given the day off work and who had turned out for the ceremony more out of curiosity for the spectacle than out of love for the deceased. And yet, this woman who was devoid of particular qualities of intelligence or culture, arid of affection, restricted to her own, increasingly closed world which was made up of outward appearances and superficiality, who added nothing to the glory of the grand duchy and who, without doubt, contributed to its downfall, had, without her intention, a great merit. She brought to Florence the fabulous riches of the Duchy of Urbino in her dowry, among which were valuable collections of paintings and sculptures which today are among the most precious gems adorning the rooms in the Uffizi and the Pitti. In her will, she ordered the prized collections in her house to go to her son Francesco Maria "with the obligation, however, that at the death of the afore-said Francesco Maria, all afore-said pictures should [pass to] His Most Serene Highness, Grand Duke Cosimo, his children and descendants". And today, when proceeding through those rooms with, looking down on us from the walls, Titian's "Venus" and "La Bella", or Raphael's portraits of Julius II and Cardinal Dovizi, or Piero della Francesca's splendid images of Federico da Montefeltro, the duke of Urbino, and his wife, Battista Sforza, we cannot help but think of where they came from. Among such works are the numerous portraits of Vittoria Della Rovere painted by Justus Sustermans, court painter. Whether she is young, florid, with a supercilious air, bedecked in rich garments and precious jewels, or at a mature age, fat, flaccid, in widow's weeds and with a crucifix on her breast as in Carlo Dolci's portrait, and whether we read in her face the authority and conceit of a princess or the physical decline of a woman, we contemplate her with indulgence and we forgive her faults and her weaknesses for this gift of beauty she made to Florence.

LEA ROSSI NISSIM

MARGUERITE-LOUISE D'ORLÉANS, WIFE OF COSIMO III

First and foremost, let us glance quickly at the Florence of that time. Enclosed within the surrounding city walls (three-and-a-half ells wide, thirty ells high, interspersed with keeps) lies the evidence of the dazzling past of a city in full decline. There are no longer any signs of the wide expansion which characterised the beginning of the fourteenth century. Large areas within the limits of the "third circle" (of walls) are uninhabited or are even just fields. The four traditional bridges are more than enough to cope with the limited city traffic. The streets are still narrow and winding, bordered by small shops, with their wooden shutters and overhanging roofs to provide shelter from the rain and protect the foodstuffs from exposure to the sun. The popular centre of the city is the *Mercato Vecchio*, noisy, well-patronised and very dirty. Here condemned subjects are dealt their public lashes of the rope and thieves are exposed to public ridicule. The nearby ghetto (a mass of hovels dominated by the few old buildings left standing) is a refuge for thieves and prostitutes. A short distance away, the *Mercato Nuovo* is the economic heart of the city, where business is carried out (increasingly less of it) and which at the same time functions as a meeting point for the nobility. In the summer, however, they move on to the Cathedral where there is always a refreshing breeze to mitigate the heat of the day. There is a sense of inertia everywhere. Novelty comes late and when it does arrive is met without urgency or without any enthusiasm for renovation. The streets have not yet been illuminated and wax paper is still in use in the buildings in place of window panes which are too expensive. Rather a drab city, indeed, where daily life takes on the same tone and only brightens up on special occasions: the religious feast days of Lady Day and St John's, the arrival in town of an important personage or a princely wedding. A city in which the splendid monuments of the ages of the commune and the Renaissance do not succeed in removing that rather provincial air that has gradually been acquired, as the quarrelsome spirit of the ancient Florentines (factious if you will, but rich in initiative) has changed with the cautious desire to preserve what is left, without running any risks.

This tone of Florentine life in slow, progressive decline is also reflected in court life. On the face of it, the grand duke still has the same power and enjoys the same prestige as before. In actual fact, there is a big difference between the proud Cosimo I, audacious creator of a strong, organic state in growing territorial expansion, and the mediocre Ferdinando II, quietly inactive, conscious of the scarce, indeed inconsistent, political weight that Tuscany and the House of the Medici pull in Italy. All things considered, the grand duke is an honest, decent fellow: he tries to defend the dignity of his small state with a policy of prudent reserve and he tries to give his court a little lustre by following the advice of his brother Cardinal Leopoldo (a stronger personality than he) and displaying a certain patronage.

The grand duke's simplicity of manner and lifestyle (it would not appear entirely exact to speak about the morality of custom) contrasts with the airs that the grand duchess, the haughty Maria Vittoria Della Rovere, assumes; harsh, ambitious and rather bigoted. In the sphere of the grand ducal couple, there is Cardinal Leopoldo concerning himself with his studies, scientific experiments and religion (with an unconfessed degree of Jansenism) and Prince Mattias represents the warrior of the family. Cosimo, heir to the throne, is by now a young man. He is quite attractive to look at (only later will he tend to portliness) and has been brought up well, but he is closed in on himself, reserved and lives under the domination of his mother. Born in 1642, he is of marriageable age and, indeed, negotiations to find him a wife have been proceeding for some time now. Life at court unfolds placidly; a few soirées, a few hunting parties, some theatrical entertainment, the odd pleasure trip, many religious services and not much more.

To the city in this setting in 1661 arrived Marguerite-Louise d'Orléans. Her father, Gaston, second son of Henry IV and Marie de' Medici and the brother of Louis XIII, had first married Marie de Bourbon (from which union Anne-Marie-Louise, later known as the *Grande Mademoiselle de Montpensier,* was born) and then Marguerite de Lorraine who had given him Marguerite-Louise. The parents were two bizarre characters: he was adventurous and unstable, oscillating between plots against his brother and reconciliation with him, between some risky enterprise and humiliating peace; she, on the other hand, was eccentric and an intriguer.

Marguerite-Louise, born in 1645, had grown up and been educated in the French way: horse-riding, hunting, chit-chat, balls and a certain amount of freedom. "White, with rosy cheeks, her eyes sparkling and a great mass of hair" - such is the way Madame Gobelin describes her and this is how she appears in a youthful portrait. She was undoubtedly what today we would call a lovely girl. Perhaps she was too buxom for modern taste, but the unruly vivacity of her ways and her wayward character gave her that touch of treacherous charm which won over all doubt or reserve in those who met her. All qualities, however, which bore no weight in the complicated matrimonial conspiracies which were contrived for political ends in the courts of Europe at that time. It was, therefore, certainly not her still unripe beauty to raise the idea of uniting her with none other than her cousin, Louis XIV. Contrariwise, it was probably her father's former policies, none too straightforward and orthodox, to induce Cardinal Mazarin to scrap his project and turn his attention to the much humbler personage of Cosimo. The deal was done! Abbé Bonsi, Tuscan resident in Paris, supported the proposal which must have appeared to Ferdinando II as manna from heaven. Heavens above! The House of Medici would be related to the most powerful reigning family in Europe and her prestige, somewhat slumped at the moment, would have a lot to gain. Furthermore, from the political aspect, Tuscany would then be able to count on France's support.

So, everything was settled. It was still too soon to talk of marriage - according to an indiscretion, it would seem that the princess had not yet become a woman - but at this point there was no turning back. Thus the fate of the thirteen-year-old girl was sealed. In 1658, Abbé Bonsi presented an official request on behalf of Prince Cosimo which met with the light-hearted response of her father, "Why not? Am I not already related to the Medici by my gout?". The contract was drawn up, which was subject to the gleaning of the traditional information and which turned out to be excellent, as in any respectable marriage.

It does not seem that the princess was contrary to the marriage at the beginning, but the gossip which circulated - the rumours about the Medici and their court life which was so modest and limited compared to the one in Paris - and, perhaps, a certain pique at having lost her chance to become queen of France gave rise in her to a marked aversion to anything which smacked of Tuscany, Florence or the Medici. Then, to give added strength to this feeling, the figure of her cousin, Charles of Lorraine appeared. True love sprouted between the two young people, forming an attachment which was to last a long time and was to bring great weight to bear on Marguerite's matrimonial affairs. Nothing could be done about it. It is well-known that, against reasons of state, affairs of the heart count next to nothing. Louis XIV exercised his will and, in April 1661, the princess married Cosimo de' Medici by proxy in the chapel at the Louvre. Shortly afterwards, accompanied by a band of thirty people, including her half-sister and (just think!) Charles of Lorraine, all of whom destined to follow her to Florence, she set off for Marseilles, where Prince Mattias was waiting to lead her to (alas!) Tuscany. The farewells between the young couple in love were heart-rending. With death in her heart, the bride boarded the grand ducal galley thinking that she was, perhaps, never to see her native land again.

In this state of mind, which could hardly be defined as jovial, even less nuptial, Marguerite reached Livorno. Here another disappointment was awaiting her - the bridegroom was not there. He had come down with German measles shortly before and had had to remain hidden away in Villa Ambrogiana near Empoli as a precautionary measure. It was in this abode that the two young people met for the first time and, while Cosimo immediately fell for that gem of a girl (although, of course, he had to restrain himself under the rigid decorum which expressed his very high dignity as a prince), Marguerite, on the other hand, began to feel downright aversion for her husband, consternated as she was with her mind on France and her cousin Charles, willing herself to find everything ugly and distasteful. Not only with regard to him but also, as always happens, with regard to her mother-in-law, who felt the same way about her. That girl of "rare beauty and extraordinary vivaciousness" as the historian Galluzzi defined her, all verve and caprice, was not to the liking of the cold, haughty grand duchess who immediately saw in her daughter-in-law (and she was not mistaken) a great hazard for the tranquillity of the family and of her son, particularly.

Indeed, if a detailed secret report on relations between the couple is to be believed, troubles started on the second night. Drawn up eleven years later, this report was sent to Abbé Gondi, the Tuscan representative then in Paris, to defend Cosimo from accusations made against him at the court of France. That night, Marguerite suddenly asked her consort to put the jewels of the Crown at her disposal, thus revealing one of the many sides of her eccentric character. Caught unawares, Cosimo replied with a refusal, despite his amorous fervour. At that point, with delicate tact, the bride remarked that she had known it all along; she would have been better off married in the lowliest hut in France rather than end up in Tuscany. At this moment began the conjugal tragedy. Cosimo, who had inherited his mother's character, was torn between love and his wounded pride. To the various motives of discontent and irritation that Marguerite had brought from France with her, it is very likely that she added physical repugnance towards her husband, who, according to some, was also guilty of scarce virility. The grand duke tried to keep their variances covered up, but people were already aware of them because in October 1661, a few months after the wedding, a reverend father arrived from Paris to make peace between the two. Nothing came of it.

Quite the contrary! The situation deteriorated a year later. Cousin Charles of Lorraine turned up and, guess what! stayed quite some time in Florence. When he set off again, the princess was unapproachable and, inasmuch as she had discovered that she was pregnant, did everything she could to get rid of the baby. Without success, however (and she never did succeed, either), so that in 1663, Prince Ferdinando was born.

So began Cosimo's numerous journeys, first around Italy, then across Europe. There were no political or educational motives, but it was the grand duke's intention to mollify this rebel bride and help her to reflect in solitude

A youthful, vivacious portrait of Marguerite d'Orléans (Taddeo Baldini, Florence, Vasari Corridor).

on the fact that she just had to resign herself. Princely marriages are what they are. Why, even Ferdinando II's with Maria Vittoria Della Rovere cannot be said to have run along smooth rails. Indeed the couple had not even been together for many years and relations were chilly, yet there was no scandal. Everything appeared normal from the outside. But the grand duke had not made allowance for that devil of a character that Marguerite was; every day she got up to something new. A certain number of the people that she had brought from France were sent away and, rather maliciously, they encouraged her to get up to mischief. Out of spite, she gave Mademoiselle Bauchemont eight fine pearls belonging to the Crown. General alarm, a rapid chase and the pearls were finally retrieved at Lyons.

News of conjugal disaccord continued to rain down on Paris, provoking a spate of gossip at court. Louis XIV sent one ambassador after the other to placate the unruly princess and, in the end, he decided to send Madame Du Deffand who, having attended to the education of her half-sister, the *Grande Demoiselle*, was perhaps the ideal person to persuade her. All was in vain. Indeed, when Cosimo returned from his first journey and showed up in his wife's bedroom as a dutiful husband should, he was greeted with the warning that "if he dared come back once more she would throw something at him".

Another melancholic departure of the prince and this time the princess was confined to the villa at Poggio a Caiano, where she was left on her own to meditate on her wrong-doing. Every now and then it seemed that the isolation had had its effect; in July 1664, she herself made an attempt at conciliation, but she put forward her conditions and a week later proceedings were back at square one again. Finally, in 1665, there was a big scene; the princess threw herself into her husband's arms (on his return from his second journey), sobbed and begged forgiveness. The state of peace was marked with a new pregnancy. But when Anna Maria Luisa, the future Electress Palatine, was due to be born, clouds once more collected over the Medicean couple. Marguerite engaged in all kinds of bizarre actions. She was on cordial terms (too much so) with a Frenchman of low condition and she consorted closely with some Gypsies at Pisa. It was even feared that she would run away with them. Where to? To Germany, by Jove! Why was she studying German so willingly while she showed no liking for the Italian language? Far away in the background loomed the shadow of her German cousin, Charles of Lorraine, and it is a shadow which, was understandably becoming a right nuisance for her legitimate consort. Grand Duke Ferdinando resorted to the usual expediency; he sent his son out of Tuscany on a third long journey which took in several European capitals. The prince's return was less stormy and there followed a calmer period, a kind of armistice. But, meanwhile, in 1670, Ferdinando II died. The fact that this unfortunate marriage had survived as well as it possibly could was due to him.

Cosimo became grand duke. Though his mother lived separately from him, she was now freer to guide her son. She watched over him, followed him, felt he was just like her - a mixture of pride, vanity and conceited superciliousness, together with a superficial, restricted religiousness - but she realised that he was still tied by a fine thread of love to his eccentric, capricious wife, and she tried to loosen the knot. Meanwhile, a third child, Gian Gastone, had been born, the last scion of the House of the Medici and also the last of this ill-assorted union.

The final crisis, kept secret, exploded belatedly in 1672. One day, Marguerite, now grand duchess, went on a visit to Poggio a Caiano. When she got there, she announced that she would return to Florence no more. And so began the de facto separation of the two. The letters exchanged between husband and wife on that occasion were significant. She wrote, "I can no longer live with you. I am the source of your unhappiness as you are of mine". Cosimo answered, "I do not know if your unhappiness could have exceeded mine". The grand duchess wrote even more explicitly to Louis XIV that she had left the Grand Duke, that she did not love him and never would. How could she possibly live with a man who had deceived her fifty times as indeed she had done, too? She wished to return to France, it mattered not where, and retire to a convent. Only in this way could she regain her lost serenity.

Thus began the period of the grand duchess's seclusion. She could not receive people at her villa without the authorisation of the grand duke; no-one in her retinue could travel from Poggio a Caiano to Florence without permission; gatherings, entertainments and peasant dances on the premises were forbidden. The grand duchess was attended by two gentlemen, Lucio Malvezzi and Andrea Minerbetti, who seemingly were at her service, but in truth were there to keep an eye on her and prevent her from talking to anybody on the sly. They also were to study her reactions when she received and read her post and to give a day-by-day report on her movements, what she did and what she said. This harshness was not justified merely by Marguerite's decision to separate from her husband, but also by another fact which had exacerbated the situation. A letter from cousin Charles containing expressions of love fell into Cosimo's hands and the latter, who had closed an eye on certain "low-class" tendencies of his wife, felt decidedly offended now that her betrayal had been consumed (at least in her mind) with one of his own social class. All relations with Marguerite were broken off; an ancient love had turned into unquenchable loathing.

Meanwhile, back in Paris, the grand duchess's desperate appeal had aroused much bafflement. How could a public separation of the grand ducal couple possibly be allowed? The scandal would be enormous. Marguerite had to be persuaded that it was not feasible. And so a more authoritative messenger was sent, Monseigneur Serre, Bishop of Marseille, accompanied by the same Madame Du Deffand. When the arrival of the two envoys was announced, their intentions being evident, the grand duchess affected indifference. She could be heard singing all day long, but, as Andrea Minerbetti wrote in one of his daily reports, "although she laughed and tried very hard, she could not stop her tears from falling".

So began the long sittings to try and get Marguerite to go back on her decision to abandon her husband. They were unpleasant sittings lasting for hours and hours, broken by an outing or two, a country dance - intervals needed in the long, fruitless task of persuasion on the part of Mgr. Serre and Mme. Du Deffand.

One evening a messenger arrived from France. Lucio Malvezzi wrote: "Great cheer at dinner; wherefore among the good news communicated in the letters brought from France and the greetings from the Bishop to his Serene Highness on behalf of the people at [the French] Court, any person who had ever thought of it previously would have been eager to go and enjoy those happy places." A charming picture! One can just imagine the scene. Forgetting their differences for a moment, the Grand Duchess, the Bishop and Mme. Du Deffand were all united in a glittering evocation of scenes, parties, people and gossip of the Sun King's Court. In their minds' eye, they were all in France; Marguerite with her nostalgia and the others secure in the knowledge that they would soon immerse themselves once more in that world of gleeful magnificence. The Italians who were present, listening, felt out of the conversation, excluded from that phantasmagorical country opening up before their eyes. One can almost hear Lucio Malvezzi grumbling into his chin, "To the devil with the Grand Duke! If Her Serene Highness manages to escape to France, I think I'll go after her - to Paris!". Because deep down, he also was charmed by that woman. Any attempt at persuasion was in vain. Marguerite would not go back on her decision. The Bishop and Mme. Du Deffand could only set out on their return journey without having achieved anything.

The months passed and at last, in 1674, Cosimo III and Louis XIV came to an agreement - the grand duchess was to return to France, shut herself up in the convent at Montmartre and emerge only with the king's permission. Cosimo was to pay eighty thousand French livres annually.

Family farewells were rather chilly and formal, even as far as her children were concerned. Marguerite had never felt much love for them. In her contorted way of reasoning, she considered that the marriage was not valid and therefore the children did not belong to her but only to her consort. The latter, indignant because of the domestic events, decided that he would not go with the other members of the family to say goodbye. So it was that, just before boarding the ship, the grand duchess wrote to him from Livorno. She begged his forgiveness for the trouble she had caused him, but at the same time she declared that she herself was ready to forgive her husband's faults. And this infuriated His Serene Highness, who, if he had followed the wise advice of his representative in Paris, would have kept quiet and would have bothered his head no more about Marguerite. Quite the opposite! Cosimo got het up, he sent people to keep an eye on her, he kept himself informed of every movement that the grand duchess made and of her friendships, ending up by increasingly irritating his consort. In actual fact, she left the convent when and for how long she felt like, she visited the royal court, she recounted the life in Florence in her own way, she heaped ridicule on the grand duke, creating a hostile environment for him which reflected on his relations with Louis XIV. Marguerite's conduct, meanwhile, was a perpetual contradiction. Her bouts of uncontrolled anger were followed by outbursts of headlong generosity or jocund merriment; she ran to look after the sick in hospital; she made arrangements for sermons to be preached, fervently following them. But she also went from one love affair to another, all of them low-class, and she threw her money around extravagantly.

All this was well-known to Cosimo, who wrote and re-wrote to Louis XIV. He complained that the pacts had not been respected. He protested that his wife behaved appallingly and that she spent too much. The Sun King smiled at first and then got rather annoyed and finished up replying to the grand duke that he must pay her debts and leave him alone. He was under no obligation to exert control over the personal tastes of his cousin.

And Cosimo made himself sick with anguish, so much so that he drove himself to the point of death. This gave his wife the idea of taking over the grand duchy and sending her mother-in-law, Maria Vittoria, away for good and turning Tuscany into a carefree offshoot of Paris and Versailles. Her plans, however, soon fell through because Cosimo regained his health in full and took up close surveillance of his wife once more. Exasperated, she picked up her pen one day and wrote the famous letter: "I can no longer put up with your extravagances. I know that you are doing your utmost to turn the King against me. You are harming your own children as well as me and yourself, because you are driving me into such a state of despair that no hour of the day passes when I do not desire your death and wish that you were hanged. You have reduced me to such a state that I may no longer receive the Sacraments and in this way I will be doomed as you will be doomed, too, for all your devoutness....What aggravates me most of all is that we shall both go to the devil and then I shall have the torment of seeing you even there...I swear by what I loathe above all else, that is yourself, that I shall make a pact with the devil to enrage you and to escape your madness. Enough is enough, I shall engage in any extravagance I so wish in order to bring you unhappiness...If you think you can get me to come back to you, this will never happen, and if I came back to you, beware! because you would never die but by my hand".

The letter was written in one of her unwarranted fits of rage. But she repented the following day, recognised she was in the wrong and charged her confessor to forward her excuses.

Her life was agitated even there among the walls of Montmartre, where an indulgent prioress managed at first to keep her fairly calm by keeping an eye closed. When, however, the superioress was succeeded by someone stricter, there was real trouble. A fire broke out one night and Marguerite was suspected of having caused it as an excuse for moving out of the convent. Which is what did indeed happen shortly afterwards. But at this point Louis XIV had had enough and, under the influence of Père La Chaise, forbid her presence at court, while leaving her amply free to give vent to her constant state of agitation.

Her last son, Gian Gastone, had married Anne of Saxe-Lauenburg against his will and had been compelled to live in Bohemia. Bored with his country life and desperate in his loneliness, he tried to escape his sad "prison" by undertaking a journey throughout Europe in 1698 and, naturally, he turned up in Paris.

Some historians have gone to town over this point. His meeting with his mother is described romantically as full of tears and desperation. But, on the contrary, to go by the usual informants, it would seem that Marguerite's welcome for her son was extremely cool. It all boiled down to one visit and an invitation to lunch. Perhaps the sight of her son awakened in the old lady memories of an unhappy past, or there again his presence may have rekindled her sentiments of hate against his father. We cannot penetrate her innermost feelings. It seems, however (still according to informants), that Gian Gastone was deeply disappointed. He had hoped to receive words of sympathy and understanding on the failure of his marriage, but he obtained nothing. It appears that, feeling very dejected, he consequently anticipated his departure from Paris. But these were just the final outbursts of a troubled soul which only the passage of years could dominate. She went on living for a long time, did Marguerite; it was only in 1721 that her long existence came to a close.

A complex figure, with a passionate self-interest. Intense and extravagant, violent and generous, crotchety, sensual, always spontaneous, with no inhibitions, Marguerite-Louise d'Orléans was clinically defined by Gaetano Pieraccini as "a great hysteric". And it has to be admitted that his judgement is exact. Basically, she was unhappy. She may be the object of sympathy, contempt, comprehension or misery, but a historical judgement can never be pronounced on her - it would not be fair.

SERGIO CAMERANI

ANNA MARIA LUISA DE' MEDICI
ELECTRESS PALATINE*

So, we have discovered who Cosimo III's wife, Marguerite-Louise d'Orléans, was and what she was like. Despite the fact that she did not like her husband (indeed she loathed him), she bore him three children: two boys, Ferdinando (born in 1663) and Gian Gastone (born in 1671) and a girl, Anna Maria Luisa (born in 1667). The Medici family succession seemed to be guaranteed. But in actual fact, that great family was nearing the end, almost as if its vitality had gone sour and dried up. Ferdinando and Gian Gastone had no heir called Medici and neither had Anna Maria Luisa a child to whom the Tuscan crown could pass eventually.

Anna Maria Luisa saw the light in Palazzo Pitti in Florence on 11 August 1667. Four years after the first-born Ferdinando and four years before the last, Gian Gastone. Standing as godparents to her were Cardinal Leopoldo de' Medici and her aunt on her mother's side, Anne-Marie-Louise d'Orléans, from whom she got her name. She was a normal, healthy baby and a lovely, dark-haired, vivacious and intelligent child. Marguerite-Louise d'Orléans-Medici obviously had no normal maternal instincts, or perhaps it was her repulsion for her husband which cancelled out any she might have had. In fact, in July 1675 that "irate soul" left Tuscany, Florence, her husband and her children for good. Ferdinando was twelve, Anna Maria eight and Gian Gastone four. This desertion clearly weighed heavily on the formation of Ferdinando and Gian Gastone's muddled temperaments. Left in the hands of tutors who had little authority and scarce sensitivity, they suffered from the lack of a mother's guidance and tenderness, and their developing spirits and characters were not steered in the right direction. Their mother's final flight must have seemed to them, innocent as they were, a bitter, unjust abandonment. Their parents' indubitable rows and the whispered comments and mockery of the court must have reached their ears and must have been the cause of the grievances that they always bore.

Perhaps the only positive thing inherited from their mother was, in all three children, their love for music and a well-defined musical temperament. All of them played an instrument and could sing. Ferdinando stood out among them, and he seems to have played a not insignificant role in the evolution

---

* We have a good deal of information about the Electress Palatine. This is mostly due to Gaetano Pieracini and especially to an erudite, impassioned German researcher, Doctor Hermine Kuhn-Steinhausen, authoress of many works concerning this princess.

particularly of opera. Gian Gastone accompanied his sister Anna Maria on the guitar and at seven she could already play an instrument and sing. In fact, it is said that she always sang very well.

Anna Maria Luisa was luckier in her childhood and youth than her brothers were because she grew up under her paternal grandmother, Vittoria Della Rovere-Medici, who was extremely fond of her and gave a proper, upright direction to her life which never let her down. The obese old lady, the Dowager Grand Duchess had great influence at court. Her extremist religiousness, too frequently expressed in an outward form, degenerated in her son, Cosimo III, into almost maniacal, obsessive and petty bigotry. The young princess was indeed very religious herself and the forms her religion took were often habit-bound and skin-deep, according to the custom of the times. But still, at the bottom of her heart, she always remained a steady, sincere believer ... and in difficult moments, she truly acted as a believer.

Her father and grandmother brought her up beautifully. We know that the young princess was very scrupulous and a stickler for hygiene. She loved flowers which she kept in her bedroom, too. She was always keen on the open air life, just as she liked exercise and long walks which made her very strong and indefatigable. Apart from teaching her music, singing, dancing and exquisite manners (to good advantage, too) her father and grandmother set great store on making a cultured princess out of her. Thus it was that she studied Latin and modern languages very well and she was interested in literature. She also loved art and beautiful things as almost all the Medici did. She could write confidently and with the steady, elegant hand of those accustomed to writing a lot. Hundreds of her letters can still be found nowadays, especially in the Florentine Sate Archives. There transpires a constant, sincere attachment to the family from all of them.

She loved Florence and Tuscany passionately. Conveyed by events to live at a distance, she kept them in her heart as a very live and comforting presence, continually mentioning them in her letters.

She always felt a great deal of affection for her uncle, Cardinal Francesco Maria, Cosimo III's brother. That pleasure-loving, superficial personage clearly felt tenderness and comprehension for his niece (apart from the fact that he felt the same for Gian Gastone, who was ignored by everyone) and, seeing as the princess had a high-spirited, playful character, he managed to show her those better, more positive aspects of the serene life that unfolded in his villa at Lapeggi, which he had had sumptuously rebuilt. He evidently hid the obscure, controversial areas of that pomp and allowed her to see only the beautiful side. Accordingly, the hours and days spent at Lapeggi remained for her something precious and almost perfect. Her soul was therefore gratefully bound to her serene uncle who was of almost the same age and was so different from those boring people who surrounded her at court in Florence, all gloomy, dissatisfied, serious and bigoted. She constantly wrote to her uncle when she was away, informing him of the developments in her life and impishly calling him "my dear priest" and "my dear, gouty priest". With playful familiarity, she even came out with expressions like, "I bow down to your handsome paunch".

Anna Maria had enormous affection for her father, Cosimo III. She was, of course, always the favourite among the three children. Letter upon letter written from her distant abode to her "very beloved father" were devoted to keeping him informed on the goings-on in her life, always trying to show him the positive side and tranquillise him as far as she was concerned.

Anna Maria learned those manners and that countenance which, according to late seventeenth-century ideas, a princess of a reigning family should have. So it was that, when she reached an age considered suitable for marriage - which, at that time, parents and diplomats regularly arranged between very young members of the great families (often even when just children) - she was the perfect princess, destined to climb very high. In actual fact, the Medici family had already had two queens of France. It was logical that Cosimo should go to great lengths to marry his favourite daughter off to a king, too, opening negotiations in various courts and doubtlessly circulating miniature portraits of her among eligible bachelors, along with information full of praise on her virtues and, of course, on her dowry, as was fitting in similar circumstances.

So we are filled with curiosity to find out what she was like, this Anna Maria Luisa, daughter of Grand Duke Cosimo III of Tuscany and Marguerite-Louise d'Orléans. Her contemporaries had this to say about her. In 1648, when she was seventeen, the ambassador from Lucca, G. Paolo Bonvisi, said that she had "a flourishing complexion and a fine bearing if it were not for eyes. She is imposing, with heavy features and sings well". Foucher, the French ambassador at the court of Florence described her when she was twenty-two as "one of those beauties that develop as they grow; the older she gets the lovelier she becomes - *C'est une vraie romaine d'une grande taille fine et droite*". He said that she had black hair and a rosy complexion and was rather *embonpoint,* adding "and a day does not pass without her appearing more beautiful. For a long time her eyes had no expression, but today they have fire and spirit. She walks with much grace, though perhaps with a little too much haughtiness. She dances very well, can ride like a man and shoots with such skill that she could compete with anyone. She is bursting with health and has extraordinary resistance to fatigue, nothing troubles her, nothing upsets her, she can eat absolutely anything. Her servants have never heard her complain about anything. This young princess, a delight to her father and of whom her younger brother is very fond, is inscrutable, as all who approach her assert. She affects such a show of indifference to everything that nobody has managed to discern her inclinations or recognise in her a "penchant" for anybody. This goes to indicate that one day she will be an accomplished princess. She has spirit, she loves literature and has a perfect knowledge of music. She knows many languages thoroughly, but she speaks so little that nothing transpires on the outside about what she actually does know. She has been brought up by her grandmother... She is deemed to go a long way and the granddaughter's merits will obscure her grandmother's". A hand-written biography of her, dating from the same year of her death at the age of over seventy-five years in 1743, which is kept in the State Archives in Florence describes her (in a rather fawning manner, admittedly) as "gifted with a beauty and grace out of the ordinary, with a sublime, serious and diligent spirit, and with all the other virtues which become her sex and which correspond to any higher and more fortunate standard".

It is known that Anna Maria Luisa loved jewellery on which she spent enormous sums, even though she always received a lot in gifts from her father and husband. We are told by some contemporaries that, as a bride, she had as many as a queen. An eye witness at her wedding in 1691 says that she was "extraordinarily fond of pomp and very dignified. She was tall, with a fair complexion and had large, expressive eyes, as black as her hair. Her mouth was small, with full-blown lips, and her teeth as white as ivory. She had a masculine voice and a loud laugh".

Many portraits exist of her and some sculptures, too - one of them is at Düsseldorf, the work of Gabriele Grupello, court sculptor. But a lot of the paintings of her were due especially to Adriano Van Der Werff and Jan Frans van Douven, the court painter at Düsseldorf. Many of these are now in Florence: at the Uffizi, the Palatine Gallery and in the Vasari Corridor.

As we were saying, Cosimo was aiming high for her marriage. There were lengthy negotiations which turned out unsuccessfully for various reasons (not least of all, her dowry) with the House of Savoy, the King of Portugal and Louis XIV, who would willingly have had her for the Dauphin (but apparently plans for this wedding were turned upside down by the constantly bellicose Marguerite-Louise d'Orléans, jealous of her daughter's potentially greater power). Even James II of Great Britain and the Austrian Emperor were involved in trying to find her a husband. It was the latter to suggest that she marry the Elector Palatine of the Rhine, Johann Wilhelm. Finally, the long, particularised negotiations reached their goal and turned out satisfactorily.

Wilhelm was nine years older than Anna Maria Luisa and had been left a widower with no children. He was the brother of two queens (of Portugal and Spain) and of one Empress (of Austria); consequently he enjoyed a position which was politically and socially very important, as well as the right to regal honours. He was very rich and at the head of a brilliant court. He had all the qualities Cosimo III could have wished for in a son-in-law. He was, furthermore, cultured, a music- and art-lover (his collections of figurative art at Düsseldorf were among the most beautiful in Europe and in part went to make up the *Pinakothek* in Munich). He was lively, dedicated to the sports of the time (hunting, fishing, horse-riding and so on), tidy and clean. And serene, too. He was not at all handsome to our present-day taste. And the portliness which weighed him down in his mature years certainly did not improve matters. But Anna Maria de' Medici never complained of this aspect, or so it seemed. There are a great number of portraits of him, too. And particularly interesting among these (considered from the aspect of the history of costume for both him and her) are the ones at the Pitti Gallery, showing them at a ball and dressed in all their finery.

Having officially requested Cosimo III for the hand of Anna Maria on 15 November 1690 and having sent the bride precious gifts of jewels (she was, unfortunately, in bed with chilblains when they arrived), the Elector Palatine thus settled his marriage plans and the wedding was celebrated in great style on 21 April 1691 in the Cathedral in Florence. It was, of course, by proxy, as was the custom when residence was to be taken up some distance away and if the bridegroom did not bother to make the journey. Ferdinando, the bride's brother, represented the bridegroom. The document certifying the marriage was underwritten by various important names of the Florentine aristocracy: Salviati, Corsini, Panciatichi, Ricciardi and others. There were parties, balls and farewell receptions, then came departure from her family, from her adored father and grandmother, from her brothers, from her beloved Florence, from Tuscany. On 6 May, Anna Maria Luisa, now officially the Electress Palatine, set off in the direction of Germany.

From letters in the princess' own handwriting and reports of various people in her retinue or diplomats, we can follow her journey almost hour by hour. It took fifteen days to get from Florence to Düsseldorf, seat of the Elector. Gian Gastone, then eighteen, accompanied her as far as Verona. At that point, her Italian retinue (in which there was a confessor, a doctor, a surgeon, many servants and her nurse, who had come on her grandmother's insistence) was joined by the German one which included Count Hamilton. Her first lady-in-waiting, Dorotea Fugger, had already joined at Bologna. So the party proceeded to Innsbruck where the Dowager Queen of Poland,

Eleonora Maria, was waiting.

Meanwhile, the elector, himself a young man (he was thirty-one), could no longer curb his strong desire to reach his bride and make her acquaintance (he had kept a small portrait of her in his bedroom). Accordingly, he left Düsseldorf before he had originally planned and, forcing his pace (in just three days and three nights), he reached Innsbruck to receive the electress from the hands of the Queen of Poland.

Towards twelve o'clock on 25 May, Anna Maria and Wilhelm finally met in the queen's rooms. Both of them kept their silence at first. They just looked at each other without opening their mouths. They bowed and curtsied to each other. At that point Eleonora Maria broke the silence and began the conversation. The marriage vows were repeated in the queen's tiny private chapel. The *Te Deum* was sung, then everyone went to lunch which lasted until four o'clock. The princely couple retired in the evening without ceremony. The following morning they appeared towards midday, very cheerful. The electress joyfully showed the Queen the splendid *Morgengaben* she had received from the elector. More prayers, blessings, lunch and good music. After lunch, the electress sang in Eleonora Maria's room, accompanied by her husband. Gifts were exchanged, respects were paid and there was much merriment. Then the queen departed in her coach, leaving everyone with wonderful memories.

In the meantime the young bride had continually sent her news, often together with a present, to her family in Florence and she went on doing so. On 9 June, for example, she wrote to her uncle, Cardinal Francesco Maria, that she was the happiest of princesses and the most contented wife in the world. Munich, Augsburg, Neuburg and, finally, on 19 July, Düsseldorf, her ultimate home. A new country, new customs, new faces, a language she knew well, but no longer her beloved Italian language (it would seem that she never learnt to write well in German). Her husband was charming and attractive for his culture, vivacity and solicitude. Indeed, Anna Maria was jealous of him, and it seems that Wilhelm engaged in a few flirtations, such as his "certain friendship" with the daughter of one of his waiters that Neri Guadagni wrote to Cosimo III about (1711). But his wife always followed him, even at night, or so it was said.

To take for the truth what an anonymous biography written in her lifetime relates, Wilhelm gave her syphilis. If this was indeed true, we can imagine the solitary hours of terror and shame that the poor Anna Maria Luisa must have spent, once she was aware of having caught the horrible disease. She so proud, so haughty, so reserved and jealous of her intimate life. In his splendid work on the Medici of Cafaggiolo, however, Pieraccini denies this,

Anna Maria Luisa, lover of sports and the open-air, wished here to be portrayed in hunting dress (Jan Frans van Douven, Florence, Pitti Gallery).

because Anna Maria was always very healthy and strong and never gave signs of any illness of doubtful origin. We know of one pregnancy that she did not carry through (in fact, there were probably two of them, to go by the hand-written biography mentioned previously), but because of fatigue, not because of her husband's illness. After all, the Electress reached the age of seventy-five and a half without any serious or specific illness. Her death was due to cancer.

The Düsseldorf court was wealthy and full of life, and it became even more so when the elector brought his pretty, young Italian wife to that city, as she was accustomed to the ways of a court which was much more refined with regard to the life style, customs and culture. The electress soon adapted to everything, from beds to meals, so different from the Italian way of doing things. She greatly appreciated the well-heated rooms, but she suffered in the German climate. Wilhelm had the Theatre of Düsseldorf reordered (it had been designed by Mario Alberti) and Andrea Moniglia's opera *La Giocasta* inaugurated it on 12 February 1694. It should not be forgotten that Handel stayed and worked at Düsseldorf for a long time and that he went to visit Prince Ferdinando de' Medici in Florence. Moreover, the electress also knew him well. By bringing with her as her father's wedding gift Raphael's *Madonna Canigiani* (now in Munich) and other Italian works of art, Anna Maria Luisa stimulated her husband's passion for collecting art which he truly loved, as he loved all beautiful things, though his interests were more eclectic than hers.

Anna Maria also collected rarities, curios and porcelain, part of which, together with her gorgeous jewels, she kept in the cabinet given to her by her father Cosimo III that had been made in Florence on designs by Foggini (1709) and which is today in the Silver Museum in Florence, brought back to her home city when she returned as a widow.

The Düsseldorf collection of paintings became famous. A standard in the history of museology is the series of engravings by De Pigage (1778) which convey, wall by wall, its aspect with that architecture of paintings within the architecture of the rooms, of which there are only rare examples today. After various incidents, most of the Elector Palatine's collection of pictures was moved to Munich's *Alte Pinakothek*. And they were not things of little consequence, either. I shall mention but a few of the most beautiful: besides Raphael's *Madonna Canigiani* and Titian's *Holy Family* and a portrait, there are also an imposing number of pictures by Rubens - thirty-three of them - and a very important nucleus of five Rembrandts. Another example of the collecting fervour of the couple is given by the lengths the electress went to to get Rubens' gigantic *Final Judgement* which, from the

Jesuit church of Neuburg was to have been moved to the collections of the two electors. So enormous was that painting that, on giving details of its arrival in Düsseldorf to her uncle Cardinal Francesco Maria who had moved heaven and earth to get it, the Electress added that now he would have to send a room big enough to house it!

Many a time did Anna Maria write to her uncle to have him send pictures from Italy. Cosimo III also sent pictures and precious objects to Düsseldorf which aroused Anna Maria's admiration and even more so that of his son-in-law. The Electress could thus assert with pride that her collections were among the loveliest in Germany. She sincerely loved that country. But, all the same, she was still homesick for her fatherland. In her letters, she often mentioned the "Cupolone", the Petraia villa, Lappeggi... "I have been to Cologne," she wrote in 1691, "but in order to find this city beautiful I should need not to have been born in Florence".

However, being used to the strange goings-on, the bigotry and the quarrels which had marked her childhood, the Electress was enchanted with the peace of the jovial serenity of the court at Düsseldorf, such a novelty for her, and she was happy with her husband in his tender, attentive affection. This was confirmed even by Gian Gastone when he saw her again in 1707. For all the twenty-five years of their marriage, Wilhelm and Anna Maria got on very well together and were truly fond of each other. They played musical instruments and cards together, sang, went for long walks in any weather, hunted and attended parties. They also travelled abroad and around Germany, often staying in their magnificent castles.

If it is false to say that Wilhelm shared the government of his state with his wife, it is, though, true that he did not isolate her. On the contrary, he esteemed her intelligence and discernment, but Anna Maria never was a politician.

Not everything was fine at Düsseldorf, however, nor was the electress spared family vexations during her very long absence from Florence. In 1694, three years after her wedding, the woman who had been both mother and grandmother to her (she said so herself), Vittoria Della Rovere-Medici, died. Her brother, Prince Ferdinando died in 1713 - hopelessly ill, degenerate, cynical, dissatisfied, and yet much loved and mourned both by her and his young, virtuous wife, Violante of Baveria. Anna Maria had just arrived in Düsseldorf when the battles of the Thirty Years' War came so close to the city that a French invasion was feared, believed by the electress to be likely and perhaps imminent. Then with the Treaty of Ryswick, the war finished in 1697. But after a brief truce in 1701, another one broke out, this time for the Spanish succession. More danger, and very serious danger, too. All the same,

Anna Maria never left her castle in Düsseldorf, whether her husband was present or absent, even when he was far away on war or diplomatic missions. The electress never wanted to abandon those "poor people" (as she called them), even if the court ladies were dying of fright and wished to escape. She got these ladies to work for the poor and to make church paraments. Anna Maria jokingly wrote to Francesco Maria in 1703 that she was mounting guard over the Rhine, but that she would rather have done so to the Arno. In any case, she packed her most precious things up out of caution and kept them packed until 1701, when the danger of a French invasion had passed. And yet, it had come so close that the electress could follow the fighting from her castle with a telescope and she could hear the obsessive roar of the artillery nearby.

Anna Maria was very fond of her husband's family, too: her mother-in-law Elisabeth Amalia, her brothers and sisters-in-law and also her nieces and nephews. One niece, Elisabeth Augusta (the daughter of the Elector Palatine, Charles III Phillip), spent many years with her at Düsseldorf when she had been left motherless, and she received such tenderness and solicitude that she would charmingly call her "gnädige Frau Mamma".

Since time before, Wilhelm had had a kind of mania for alchemy and had been taken in by many tricksters in his Utopian search for gold. Anna Maria was well aware of this fact and she feared them and their threatening influence so much that when she once visited Vienna she secretly wrote to her mother-in-law to keep an eye on him.

On 3 February 1710, Cardinal Francesco Maria de' Medici died, that adored uncle of hers (poor man) whom, Cosimo III, in his worry about the succession, had managed to free from the purple so as to allow him to marry (he who was getting on in years) the very young Eleonora di Guastalla. This had already been done for Ferdinando I de' Medici. With the result that he brought down suffering on that poor man and the unfortunate young lady who was forced to bind her life to his (the longed-for "cousin" of the electress did not, in any case, arrive). Her uncle's death caused Anna Maria grievous sorrow. And yet that unknown biographer in 1743 wrote the following moving account which gives a measure of her strength of spirit. "It is narrated that the post from Italy arrived one winter evening at about the time that she was due to go to the theatre to hear a magnificent new opera and, when she had opened the envelope from Tuscany which she requested at once so as to have the latest news of her family and country without delay, she found the unexpected and distressing news of the death of her uncle, Prince Francesco Maria, whom she dearly loved as she loved everyone at home. Despite this, without a word to anybody so as not to deprive the elector and the court of

*The Elector and Electress
Palatine portrayed in full pomp
with their attributes of
government (Jan Frans van
Douven, Florence, Vasari
Corridor).*

*Anna Maria Luisa in a delightful
portrait by van Douven (Detail,
Florence, Pitti Gallery).*

the entertainment arranged, she closed up all the letters and went to the theatre with her usual gaiety and naturalness and she waited until her return to the palace to give any sign of her grief".

A reason for remorse, on the other hand, must have been her conscience that she had been the one to concern herself so with arranging the marriage of her brother, Gian Gastone, to Anna Maria Francesca, the widow of the Count Palatine, Philip of Neuberg. This was, of course, a marriage of convenience which took place in 1697 in the chapel of the Düsseldorf palace and which turned out to be a disaster and, furthermore, of no practical convenience, either. She was a Bohemian bumpkin, all stables, cows and horses. He, having lived in the refinery of the grand duchy, could never adapt to that rough and lonely country life. To the extent that, in trying to escape that type of existence and that kind of wife and to forget his troubles, he descended, little by little, into the most degrading depravity, losing his health, dignity and also much of the intelligence he had shown in his youth. He is one of the saddest figures among the last of the Medici. A defeated man, he returned to Florence for good in 1708, deserting his wife who never showed any inclination to follow him. And he retreated into himself, with his abominable depravities, causing grief, bitterness and shame to his sister.

In 1711, Wilhelm and Anna Maria visited Frankfurt for the emperor's coronation. Wilhelm had a heart attack that year and was very ill. But then he recovered and it seemed that everything had blown over. It is even generally known that in 1713 he returned to the opera. However, Anna Maria had no illusions as to his health, which gradually went downhill, and she was very worried about him. Indeed, when he died, he looked much older than his fifty-eight years. In 1716, Wilhelm had a serious illness, "a distressing chest complaint", as Anna Maria wrote. She never left him and for five weeks she nursed him lovingly. But the end was near. The doctors took great care of their patient and applied the drastic cures of those times, among which was blood-letting which certainly made him even weaker. He bore it all with extraordinary patience. He could neither breathe nor lie down. Comforted by the Holy Sacraments, he died on 8 June 1716. Anna Maria was at his bedside.

Although she had an extraordinary strength of spirit, the bottom fell out of her world. Her husband had represented the best part of it and she relied on him for everything. Courageously she got hold of herself and prayed on her beloved husband's coffin, which was exposed in the chapel at the palace for almost a month before being inhumed in the Jesuit church. But after that, Anna Maria gave up her mundane life and lived on prayer and pious works. She even took the initiative of a kind of spiritual exercise in public, preached by excellent orators.

Staying in Germany had lost all attraction for her at this point. It was Florence, Tuscan and her family to lure her. She left Düsseldorf for ever on 10 September 1717, a year after Wilhelm's death, to the disappointment of the population that she had loved and assisted. The cannons rumbled in a salute. The evening prior to her departure, she had taken her final farewell from her husband's grave. He had left her handsomely provided for in his will, but, on various pretexts, Charles III never gave her the full amount owing to her. Anna Maria behaved in a very dignified manner and, and just as she had always been ready to give to her newly-adopted country, so she gave when she bade it farewell. She handed over everything which belonged to the Palatinate without taking away anything which was not strictly hers.

Two German court ladies and eighty people, servants included, accompanied her. We have minute details of her return journey also, lap by lap. She was given regal honours wherever she went, with exceptional welcomes. The journey was very slow, with long pauses between the various laps. She left Trento on 6 October. She had met up with a splendid escort which had been sent by her father and which Gian Gastone scorned. It may be said that it was at this moment that his stubborn hostility against his sister began. It was probably the deep grudge that he bore her for the part that she had played in that very unfortunate marriage which had ruined his life and had reduced him to the poor, solitary desperate depraved man he had become.

Big names of the Florentine nobility - Ginori, Gerini, Quaratesi, Guadagni, Antinori and others - came to meet her. About thirty people in her German retinue continued the journey with her. They gradually passed through those places that she had left behind twenty-six years previously. The legate Cardinal Origo extended to her a stately welcome to Bologna. We suppose that her anxiety to get to Florence grew and grew. On 21 October 1717, after twenty-six years, Anna Maria stepped onto Tuscan soil. Gian Gastone came to meet her at Scarperia, not having seen her for twenty years. The morning after, there arrived Violante, widow of Prince Ferdinando, and Eleonora di Guastalla, widow of Prince Francesco Maria. After lunch they moved on to Florence. Gian Gastone rode next to the carriage which was bringing his sister back.

Next came the shots of welcome. There were also shots from the great cannon "San Paolo", now in the Bargello Museum. They came down the hill and entered the city through the Porta San Gallo. And here was Anna Maria at the "Santissima Annunziata", at the foot of Our Lady of the Annunciation, patron saint of Florence. Cosimo III, her father, was waiting in the chapel of the cloisters and with deep emotion he would not let her kneel before him but hugged her instead.

Anna Maria tarried a while in prayer. Cosimo returned to the Pitti. And when she got there, he was waiting for her with Violante and Eleonora at the bottom of the main staircase. She was assigned the apartments of her grandmother Vittoria, which today are called the Volterrano Suite, included in the Palatine Gallery. So it was that, after so long an absence, his favourite daughter was living near him and he could go and visit her twice a day. The grand duke's rooms were at the back of the Palatine Gallery (the present-day *Sala della Stufa* and *Sala di Prometeo*).

So began the electress' new life in Florence. She and Wilhelm had put their hearts into doing everything possible to favour Tuscany. For example, they once managed to halve a heavy duty imposed on Cosimo by the emperor, and it is thanks to Wilhelm if Cosimo was granted the title of Royal Highness and regal honours (which he eagerly desired). But the electress had hardly any of her previous power left to her. Her haughtiness and high-handedness - the negative side of her character, mostly inherited from Cosimo III and Vittoria Della Rovere - were inborn in her and had been increased by the eminent position enjoyed by her in the Palatinate until a short time previously, ratified by the recent grandiose regal welcomes on her way home. With the result that she entered into conflict with Violante of Baveria, the widow of her elder brother Ferdinando (he had died four years previously). She expected homage to be paid to her and Violante to be subordinated. To her delight, the solution found for this royal squabble (not very regal, in truth) was the following: Anna Maria was to stay in Florence and Violante was sent to Siena as Governor, staying there until her death, making a good show of her excellent qualities as, after all, the valid princess had always done.

As she did not have a villa to herself, Anna Maria had an apartment put at her disposal in the convent at la Quiete. Here she spent her summers. But, apart from the episode mentioned above, she behaved beautifully and tried to make herself useful to the Florentines who applied to her to obtain help and favours. In fact, cynical Gian Gastone said that Florence had three Madonnas; one of grief (Violante), one of milk (the fat Eleonora di Guastalla, Francesco Maria's widow) and the third of grace (Anna Maria).

There was nothing in her demeanour to arouse objections. A *Vita* written in her lifetime and published by Baccini in 1890 describes her life in her last years (and it was certainly not a biography compiled by a person who was benevolent and obsequious towards her); "The Princess Electress leads a well-regulated life. Rarely does she leave the palace in the morning and later on in the day she partakes of the Most Holy Sacrament on her rounds for the Forty Hours' Devotion and then the usual churches where various saints' feasts are celebrated. She always lunches and dines at the same time".

Further on, it says, "Her greatest delight is in jewellery and also a little in ancient and modern paintings, of excellent composition...It is therefore believed that she will live a long time"! The unknown biographer does not, however, consider her genuinely limitlessly charitable, but rather with a disparity of treatment between nobles and the rest.

Hence her life is sad and monotonous, the complete opposite of what is was like at the lively court of Düsseldorf. The electress kept two constant loves in her heart: that for her family and that for Florence and Tuscany. Cosimo III would have liked Anna Maria to succeed him. Indeed, almost immediately after her return, he made reference to an old regulation from the times of Cosimo I and had this ordinance ratified by the Senate and the Council. He received a sign of approval from the emperor. But this accounted for little. On account of the fact that Gian Gastone was inept, debauched and a sick man, the problem of the succession in the Tuscan Grand Duchy was a very topical one. Too many people claimed kinship with the Medici and consequently their right to the succession.

The Quadruple Alliance of Hanover decreed that Tuscany should go to the Spanish Infante, Prince Don Carlos (later to become Charles III), with the pretext that Tuscany (Siena essentially) was a Spanish feud. With similar reasoning, Austria asserted that it was, instead, an imperial feud. In any case, Anna Maria was to be excluded because, apart from the fact of being a woman, she had no children. Neither did Gian Gastone have any offspring. The unfortunate idea of using Francesco Maria was not fruitful, either.

Perhaps, as it has rightly been said, this anguish at seeing Tuscany finish up in the hands of foreigners and, moreover, the knowledge that the House of the Medici was dying out, shortened Cosimo III's life. Following a severe infection which he lacked the strength to fight, he died on 31 October 1723. He was a controversial and much-discussed figure, wretched in himself and in respect of others, tormented and oppressive, all shadows and light, though perhaps more shadows than light.

The new Grand Duke Gian Gastone was not generous with Anna Maria. He did not even want to recognise as legitimately hers her rights to the allodial assets of their grandmother Vittoria Della Rovere that the dying Cosimo III had indicated as belonging to her. It was again that deep grudge in the bottom of his heart, holding her responsible for his exceedingly unhappy marriage, arranged by his sister with such poor long sightedness so many years previously. The docile and virtuous Violante, Governor of Siena, died in 1731. But Gian Gastone would not allow Anna Maria to take her place or use the villa at Lapeggi which had been assigned to Violante and which was so dear to the electress.

Peace between Spain and the emperor freshly changed Tuscany's destiny. The grand duchy went to Francis III of Lorraine instead of to Charles III of Spain, as an indemnity for the loss of Lorraine which had to be ceded to Poland. And on 9 July 1737, the unhappy life of the last Medicean grand duke, was also extinguished - that inept, debauched Gian Gastone. Forgetting the insults she had received, Anna Maria had assisted him lovingly. He had dragged the Medici name very low in a final, pitiful downfall.

Just three days later, the Senate and the Council of Florence put the pledge of allegiance into the hands of Francis of Lorraine. For the time being, Anna Maria was to hold the regency until the arrival of the new sovereign. The meeting between the electress and the Lorrainer grand duke and his wife, Maria Theresa (the future famous Austrian empress) took place on 20 January 1739 and was cordial, deferential and friendly. The electress allowed Maria Theresa to use some of the famous Medicean jewels. And she agreed to be godmother to the little Grand Duchess Maria Anna. The young grand ducal couple begged her to remain in the apartments assigned to her in Palazzo Pitti by her father and to concern herself with the state in their absence. But she was old, discouraged and tired. While Francis and Maria Theresa in that same year were visiting Siena, she noticed the first symptoms of cancer in her left breast. Deeply perturbed at the bottom of her heart, she pulled herself together and gave no clue as to her condition either to them or to anyone else, keeping it hidden from her own doctor almost until the last moment and getting her faithful chambermaid Maria to medicate her without letting anyone know.

Once Gian Gastone had died, the electress' last cares concentrated on the two great passions of her life: the Medici family and Florence with Tuscany. She realised that only by binding these two loves tightly together in one whole could she bring benefit and everlasting glory to her country and to the Medici. So it was that she bound the immense *private* (and not grand ducal) assets of the Medici indissolubly to Tuscany (and not, as Acton suggests, out of petty sentiments of spite and jealousy, either). These had remained in her possession alone. Immediately after her brother's death, she spoke of her wishes to Francis of Lorraine and came to an agreement with him.

And so, as required by the directive, she nominated to this end her plenipotentiary in Vienna, *Marchese* Bartolommei, while the new grand duke nominated his plenipotentiary, Baron Pfutschner. Negotiations were begun immediately and gave rise to the famous "Family Pact", signed in Vienna by the two plenipotentiaries on 31 October 1737. The third article was the one that for Florence signified public possession of the immense artistic and cultural heritage of the Medici. This is why we venerate the memory of the Electress Palatine; she gave to Florence for eternity the treasures of her collections which have made the city famous and unique the world over. "Article III: With the present act, Her Very Serene Highness, the Electress bequeaths that all furniture, effects and rarities from the estate of HSH her brother, including galleries, paintings, statues, libraries, jewels and other valuable things, such as holy relics, reliquaries and their hangings in the chapel of the Royal Palace, be transferred to HRH the Grand Duke and his successors, and that HRH shall undertake to keep them on the express condition that they are to serve both the state, for the benefit of the public, and to arouse the interest of foreigners, and none of it may be removed from the capital and the state of the Grand Duchy. The household linen, silverware and personal effects will remain at HRH's free disposal."

And she confirmed this in her will of 5 April 1739 with regard to the jewels that would be part of her legacy, saying that they were to be joined to the State collection and they should be used as ornaments for the Serene Grand Dukes and Grand Duchesses reigning in Florence and that they were all to be perpetually conserved in the city of Florence together with all the statues, pictures, medals and other rare curios which she had found in the family inheritance. The validity *in perpetuum* of this will and the Family Pact allowed the recuperation from Austria in 1919, after the end of the First World War, of some of the electress' jewels which had been illicitly removed to Vienna by the Lorraines. Today they are conserved in the Silver Museum at Palazzo Pitti. These jewels had immediately aroused Austrian aspirations and two officers had even tried to take them away by force when the electress was old and alone.

Furthermore, the electress wanted to bring to completion a work that had been the wish of her family which was the building of the *Cappella dei Principi* (Medici Chapel) for the Medicean burials in the Church of San Lorenzo and the restoration of the same church. The architect Ruggeri was the one she turned to. The dome of the Chapel (painted by Meucci) was reinforced as were the church ceiling (which the electress had restored and gilded), the bell tower, the lantern and the terraces around the smaller dome. The pilasters were strengthened and the vaults, tombs and the floor of the cemetery under the church restored. When work was under progress on the dome, Anna Maria herself was wont often to go almost to the top to check up on the work. But the *Cappella dei Principi* and its altar were not finished.

Her illness took its course. Old age weakened the princess more and more. In the end, the electress had to confess her illness to her doctor Franchi.

At the end of 1742 she felt death was near. Extending her hands, she would exclaim "My life is coming to an end!". She could no longer walk. She had to be carried to the chapel in a wheel chair.

In February 1743, there was a severe 'flu epidemic in Florence. It can be surmised from accounts quoted by Pieraccini that the electress also caught it and then it degenerated into acute bronchopneumonia. She coughed and suffocated. Death was at the door. In the late evening of 18 February 1743, Anna Maria Luisa de' Medici gently gave up the ghost in the Pitti Palace. She rests in the Church of San Lorenzo.

She has been very severely judged by some, others heaping rather exaggerated praise on her; 'hosanna-ed' and 'crucified'. It happens to many and especially the powerful. But if we stop to consider the good that this woman did even to the humble people close to her, I believe we may mitigate slightly the definite judgement passed on her pride and superciliousness. Let us remember that at Pisa she once donned a nurse's apron in the hospital and tended and fed the sick. Finally, let her be remembered for the generous gift of all the Medicean collections that she made Florence. After all, when all is said and done, we, too, are among her beneficiaries.

ANNA MARIA FRANCINI CIARANFI